KEY TO AN ENIGMA

KEY TO AN ENIGMA

British Sources Disprove British Claims to the Falkland/Malvinas Islands

Angel M. Oliveri López

LYNNE
RIENNER
PUBLISHERS

BOULDER
LONDON

An earlier version of this book appeared in Spanish as
Malvinas: La Clave del Enigma, published by
Grupo Editor Latinoamericano in its Colección Controversia.
© 1992 Grupo Editor Latinoamericano

Published in the United States of America in 1995 by
Lynne Rienner Publishers, Inc.
1800 30th Street, Boulder, Colorado 80301

and in the United Kingdom by
Lynne Rienner Publishers, Inc.
3 Henrietta Street, Covent Garden, London WC2E 8LU

Library of Congress Cataloging-in-Publication Data
Oliveri López, Angel M.
    [Malvinas. English. Selections]
    Key to an engima : British sources disprove British claims to the
Falkland/Malvinas Islands / Angel M. Oliveri López ; translated by
Paula Durbin ; updated and revised by the author ; with a foreword
by Wayne S. Smith.
        p.   cm.
    Includes bibliographical references.
    ISBN 1-55587-521-1 (alk. paper)
    I. Falkland Islands War, 1982—Diplomatic history. 2. Argentina—
Foreign relations—Great Britain. 3. Great Britain—Foreign
relations—Argentina. I. Title.
F3031.5.05513   1995
997'.11—dc20   94-31531
                                                            CIP

British Cataloguing in Publication Data
A Cataloguing in Publication record for this book
is available from the British Library.

Printed and bound in the United States of America

        The paper used in this publication meets the requirements
    ∞ of the American National Standard for Permanence of
        Paper for Printed Library Materials Z39.48-1984.

    5   4   3   2   1

*To my grandchildren, Stephanie, Nicholas, and those yet to arrive,
in the hope that someday in the coming century
they might leaf through this essay*

Contents

Foreword

Wayne S. Smith

Ambassador Oliveri López takes a novel approach to the dispute over the Falkland/Malvinas Islands: He uses not a single Argentine source. Rather, in shredding the British legal case, he refers to and quotes only British documents and statements, some official, others the observations of academics.

Some readers will feel he overstates the degree to which he has proved his case. Especially questionable is his repeated assertion that British "confessions" prove the Argentine case, because "one party's confession removes from the other the onus of proof." This is not a maxim recognized in Anglo-Saxon law. Confessions are frequently thrown out of court, and even with an admissible one prosecutors must still prove the rest of their case—though, of course, a confession that stands up in court does make their job a good deal easier.

Moreover, certain of the statements Ambassador Oliveri López calls "confessions" are not that at all; they are simply the expressed opinions of British academics or politicians who do not speak for the government. They may be seen as expert witnesses whose testimony bolsters the case for the prosecution rather than helping the defense. But their testimony is by no means conclusive.

Even acknowledging all this, however, it must be said that Ambassador Oliveri López, having limited himself essentially to British sources, has succeeded to a rather amazing degree in cutting the ground from under British claims to the islands. He notes, for example, that in 1834, just after the British had seized the islands, Lord Palmerston stated flatly that British rights were based on "original discovery and the subsequent occupation of those islands."

Yet a British Foreign Office note of December 17, 1982, says the British claim to first discovery is "obscure and uncertain," and goes on to insist that this "has never of itself formed the basis for our claim to sovereignty over the islands."

Virtually no one today still believes that the British, in the person of John Davis, discovered the islands in 1592. And even if they had, discovery has to be followed by occupation to have meaning. But occupation did not follow. Indeed, over 170 years passed before the British showed any further interest in the islands. Meanwhile, the Treaty of Utrecht had, in 1713, given Spain the right to control the seas and islands around its domains in the New World, and this had been confirmed by the Treaty of Paris in 1763. Thus, when the British established Port Egmont in the islands in 1766, they were trespassing on Spanish territory. Spain protested and in 1770 drove them out. True, the British were allowed to return for a short period of time, apparently to save face and avoid a war, though Spain stressed that this gesture in no way diluted its claim to full sovereignty.

True also, as the British departed again in 1774, they left behind a plaque claiming the islands for the Crown. If there was any ambiguity in the situation at that point, however, it was subsequently overcome by two things: (1) the Nootka Sound Convention of 1790, under which Great Britain acknowledged Spanish sovereignty and gave up any right to establish colonies in the southern ocean just off the mainland, and (2) British failure to make any efforts to occupy the islands between 1774 and 1833, a period of almost 60 years. If occupation is to confer title, it must be more or less uninterrupted (except in cases of force majeure). British occupation was not.

Meanwhile, sovereignty passed from Spain to Argentina, which became an independent state in 1817 (in the form of the United Provinces of the River Plate). In 1820, the new country took formal possession of the islands and in 1823 appointed Luis Vernet to set up a colony, which he did in 1826. This colony flourished until 1831, when it was disrupted by the attack of a U.S. warship, the USS *Lexington*. Colonists remained on the islands even after the attack, however, and in 1832, the government in Buenos Aires sent out a small military garrison under a Lieutenant Pinedo to reassert Argentina's authority over the islands and to give assistance to the colonists.

The British frequently assert, or suggest, that the islands were unoccupied at the time the British squadron arrived in 1833 to take them over. As Oliveri López points out, however, British records themselves refute such assertions. Captain James Onslow of the British navy called on Lieutenant Pinedo to surrender. Having no cannon or fortifications, the latter was compelled to do so. Clearly, though, this was not unoccupied territory at the time the British arrived. Argentina had clear title to it and had established a colony on it. British records themselves, while they do not so state, make it clear that this was the seizure of territory from a weaker adversary—territory that was regarded as of strategic value. This was hardly an isolated case. Land grabbing was a favorite sport of nations in the nineteenth century. The United Kingdom was not the worst offender, but also was not an exception.

As Oliveri López then goes on to point out, while British claims at the time of seizure were based on assertions of discovery and occupation prior to 1833, later reviews conducted by Whitehall pointed up the weakness of those arguments. Hence, new bases for the claims have been brought forth, and in 1982 we have Foreign Minister Francis Pym saying that British sovereignty rests not on discovery and occupation, but on "prescription and the principle of self-determination."

But these bases are no more valid than the earlier ones. True, to acquire title under the principle of prescription, a nation effectively occupies the territory over a period of time. *But the occupation must be uncontested.* If another nation claims the territory and consistently protests the first nation's occupation, then prescription goes out the window. With his usual methodology, Oliveri López cites British sources, from 1833 to the present day, that acknowledge periodic Argentine protests of British seizure and occupation. Again, it is British records themselves that destroy the case for acquisitive prescription.

The principle of self-determination is perhaps the most inapplicable of all. What we have in the Falkland/Malvinas Islands is a transplanted population. Let us imagine a hypothetical case in which the Germany of Bismarck has near the end of the last century seized the entire Jutland peninsula from Denmark, driven off its Danish inhabitants, and brought in thousands of German colonists. Denmark, of course, protests but is powerless to redress the wrong. Years pass and Denmark takes its case to a gathering of European governments called to settle disputes among them. Germany's response is to fall back on the principle of self-determination. It is, says the German foreign minister, up to the German colonists to decide whether they wish to be German or Danish!

Absurd? Of course. But no more so than to apply self-determination in the case of the Falkland/Malvinas Islands. The numbers involved and the time frame differ from our hypothetical case, but the principle is exactly the same. If all one nation had to do to legitimize its seizure of land from another was to drive off the inhabitants of the first nation, bring in its own colonists, and then claim for them right of self-determination, chaos would reign in the international community (to an even greater extent than it already does).

None of the bases for British claims, in short, are valid. The United Kingdom simply does not have a juridical case and well knows it. Oliveri López cites official British sources as acknowledging that it would be risky to take the case to court or to international arbitration. They know they would lose—or at least strongly suspect that they would. To establish that the United Kingdom has no legal claim to the islands is not, however, to solve the matter. Ambassador Oliveri López is quite realistic on that score and fully acknowledges that the matter will be resolved through a negotiated accommodation or not at all. The Islanders may not have rights of self-determination, but their wishes must be taken into account. To be fair and acceptable to all sides, any accommodation would have to allow them to continue their traditional lifestyle.

There are, however, many ways of accomplishing that objective. Oliveri López wisely calls on all sides to put aside emotion and concentrate instead on what their real interests are and how they can best advance them. At the time the United Kingdom took the islands, for example, they were of strategic value to a British empire with the mightiest fleet on the face of the globe. Today, given the United Kingdom's changed role and a drastically altered world situation, they are of no strategic value at all.

Both sides have an interest in exploiting the maritime resources of the area, but, as Oliveri López points out, they really must cooperate if they are to succeed in that endeavor. Their respective interests in the area, then, militate in favor of an accommodation, not of continued confrontation.

Oliveri López's suggested solution—divided administration under which West Falkland would pass directly to Argentine sovereignty and administration, while sovereignty over East Falkland (where the bulk of the population resides) would pass to Argentina, but with its administration remaining with the United Kingdom under a long-term leaseback— may not be the best one available, but it does point toward imaginative thinking, and that is what is needed.

In the final analysis, it seems to me that the key to this dispute is for the British to acknowledge that a wrong was done all those years ago and then through careful and patient diplomacy begin moving toward an accommodation that, while redressing that wrong, protects the basic interests of the Islanders and makes possible the effective and sensible use of the maritime resources of the area to the benefit of all sides. Not to do so is to risk, eventually, another armed conflict, and this time under circumstances in which the sympathies of the international community are not likely to be with the United Kingdom.

Preface

Much has been written about the Malvinas, but it can hardly be too much, for we are dealing here with the only national cause that truly rallies the Argentine people and that, in our time, they have consecrated with their blood.

This essay takes an original approach to the problem. Its novelty lies in the connecting thread that gives primary importance to British sources. It consists of what British politicians, parliamentarians, academics, business professionals, and, of course, the people of the islands have said and written on the Malvinas question. This is of extraordinary relevance for the Argentine case because, in keeping with an axiom as ancient as the law itself, *one party's confession relieves the other party from the onus of proof.*

It must be acknowledged that the backbone of the work—the use of material of British origin—becomes more tenuous as the text distances itself from the past and looks toward the future. So, while in the first two chapters the fabric is 100 percent English and only the "cut" is Argentine, from that point on the creative aspect of the work increases. These are personal reflections, never totally at odds with the British "confessions" but bearing my own imprint.

And why now this emphasis on British sources? Let us review a bit of history. After the United Kingdom's seizure of the islands in 1833, its foreign ministry—the renowned Foreign Office—labeled the subject "case closed," professing no doubts as to its sovereign rights, based at the time on the alleged discovery and subsequent occupation of the Malvinas. Some seven decades later, as Argentina intensified its claims, the same Foreign Office undertook an investigation of the historical events referenced. Its conclusions were reported in an initial internal memorandum written in 1910.

This document was to shake the foundations of beliefs held up to that time and to sow profound doubts in British political and diplomatic circles. These "doubts"—really proof of the flaws in its historic title—

xiii

were confirmed in later studies and produced a substantial change in the arguments advanced by the United Kingdom. As this essay reveals, the arrogantly asserted legal norm gave way to a political approach. The false mask of Themis vanished, betraying the hardened face of Power, which even today sustains the de facto exercise of British jurisdiction over the islands.

For the most part, these and other British documents on the case remained secret until the conflict in the South Atlantic and, officially, many are still classified today. Moreover, as some of them are highly sensitive, their confidentiality has been extended to 50 or 100 years. But the interest the subject has aroused has allowed private researchers, mainly British, to flout these classifications and make a substantial portion of the material public.

Furthermore, and of still greater importance, the Malvinas question—which had never figured among the British government's priorities—took on a new urgency because of an armed conflict so costly in terms of property and human lives. This was followed by official investigations. These bore on the causes of and responsibilities for the conflict and also on future British policy in the Malvinas. Two reports were issued, each particularly significant: one by Lord Franks and the other by the Foreign Affairs Committee of the House of Commons, chaired by Sir Kershaw. I will use the former as a summary of the past, prior to the conflict—15 years of bilateral negotiations—and the latter to illustrate probable alternatives for solving the controversy.

I would be remiss if I did not praise here the government of the United Kingdom, and in particular its system of parliamentary democracy, for conducting a thorough and detailed analysis and, more important, for making it public. Without these source documents this essay would have been impossible, and a substantial portion of the facts that have strained a long friendship between the two nations would not have been discovered. Argentina should undertake a similar inquiry some day—for historical purposes and not revenge—and reveal to its people the political responsibilities, both for the decision of April 2, 1982, i.e., to invade the islands, and for the handling of the crisis from that point until the surrender of Argentine forces on June 14, 1982.

For three years—from March 1978 to March 1981—as general director of the Office on Antarctica and the Malvinas in the Argentine Foreign Ministry, I shared responsibility for the formulation of the Argentine negotiating position on the southern archipelagoes: the Malvinas, the South Georgia Islands, and the South Sandwich Islands. I also participated in the bilateral discussions with the British, both Labour and Tory governments. Although I have not been involved in the subject since then, this experience made me at least a specialized observer of subsequent events and, likewise, of the parameters indicated by understandings reached as to the institutional future of the islands in the South Atlantic.

The privilege of having played a principal role in this matter of supreme national interest carries the moral obligation of sharing these experiences. I am truly convinced that this is useful now that the reopening of the negotiating process is taking shape. Negotiations will be arduous, prolonged, and not without difficulties. They will require a deep understanding of the subject and a comprehension of the other side of the story. For three years I met with British negotiators, and I must confess my ignorance at that time of at least half the information contained in these pages. Future negotiators should not be in that situation. This essay attempts to condense the essential in order to help fill the future negotiator's knapsack with the necessary provisions.

And more than that. The mere fact that the historic and diplomatic episodes of this national cause can be discovered by anyone who is interested is enough to justify the effort to record them. I am confident that this endeavor will be added to that of others from the ranks of the Argentine Foreign Ministry, the Palacio San Martín, which, while highly respected beyond our borders, is often derided by our own citizens.

In addition, in a survey taken in May 1992, both Argentines and Britishers were asked specific questions on the options for resolving the sovereignty dispute. The survey must have provoked surprise and amazement among the majority of those interviewed, who were no doubt ignorant of the backstage maneuvering in the case. Nonetheless, it is good that they should know, that they should no longer be ignorant of the facts. Not only does resurgent democracy in South America require this, but, in the final analysis, it is they, the people, who are called upon to shed their blood. They should at least know upon which altar they are called to offer their lives in sacrifice.

Angel M. Oliveri López
December 1993

Acknowledgments

I am pleased to mention here the collaboration, in one form or another, of Juan Eduardo Fleming, Colonel (Ret.) Luis González Balcarce, Mercedes Aparicio, Ernesto de la Guardia, Jr., Celia Chacón, and, especially, Helena Oliveri, my sister. Last but not least, my gratitude to Professor Wayne Smith, not only for his foreword but also for his enduring encouragement in editing the English version of this essay.

A.M.O.L.

Translator's Note

The name by which one refers to the islands that are the subject of this book can indicate a point of view. As translator, I have generally maintained the name "Malvinas" throughout the Argentine author's narrative. However, when British sources are quoted directly, their term "Falkland Islands" is used here as in the original Spanish version.

An important concept in this work is the legal maxim from civil law, the system of jurisprudence of certain countries of continental Europe and all of Latin America, expressed in Spanish as *a confesión de parte, relevo de prueba*. This has no true equivalent in common law. It implies that a party's own confession obviates the need for further proof. Outside of this limited context, throughout much of the text, *confesión* is more appropriately rendered as "admission."

The author includes at the end of his work a bibliography of 31 British sources. References to these sources are indicated throughout the text by an "S" followed by the page number in parentheses.

Paula Durbin

Preliminary Reflections
in the Form of a Prologue:
One Party's Confession Relieves the
Other Party from the Onus of Proof

Midway through a fiery address on April 3, 1982, the day after the Argentine occupation of the Malvinas Islands, British Prime Minister Margaret Thatcher declared, "We have absolutely no doubts about our sovereignty" (S. 11, p. 9). Thirty days later, Francis Pym, who would replace Lord Carrington as minister of foreign affairs stated in the midst of the crisis, "The sovereignty question is at the heart of the issue." And he ratified the Iron Lady's declaration on sovereignty, saying, "We are not in any doubt about the title to the Falkland Islands and have never been." (Ibid., p. 9)

This declaration, which we can understand in view of the political environment in which it was cast—and which was the basis for the decision to mobilize the wartime fleet and the most significant logistical support since World War II—was far from correct and does not reflect even a modicum of truth.

Peter J. Beck, professor at Kingston Polytechnic University and currently the most important British researcher of the Malvinas case, admits that his country's position changed with the Argentine occupation of the islands. Since then, opinion has it that "Britain was right and Argentina, for all its protestations to the contrary, was wrong, not only in invading the islands, but in even claiming title over them" (Ibid., pp. 8–9). Beck said that this attitude constituted "an uncritical acceptance encouraged by not only the emotions of war but also by a basic ignorance concerning the history of the sovereignty dispute" (S. 4, p. 114).

1

Confirming this assessment, I will reveal—using the words of the British—how the carefully fabricated portrayal, set forth for decades in government statements and in official publications, departs from the truth and how, on the contrary, reality casts serious doubts on their historic title to the islands. This uncertainty, which in many cases goes much further and implies virtual recognition of Argentine rights, emerges from documents and reports originating in the Foreign Office, the Colonial Office, and other ministries and sectors of government. They are classified as confidential and are therefore not available to the public or the mass media.

In an article dedicated specifically to the difficulties facing the researcher of this subject and evidently based on his own experience, Beck comments:

> In fact, material relevant to the Falkland Islands dispute is subject already to extended closure; thus, a large proportion of post-1920 records have been subject to a 50-year rule, while certain items are being placed, upon expiration of this period, upon a 75-year rule, and even a 100-year rule in some instances. (S. 9, p. 5)

But let Professor Beck explain how, these circumstances notwithstanding, he managed to compile in his latest book an exceptional collection of data:

> In spite of the obstacles placed in the way of researchers by extended closure and non-availability of files, it remains possible, nevertheless, for the researcher to piece together from the remaining files, indexes referring to the closed documents, oral evidence and overseas sources a relatively complete picture of British perceptions of the sovereignty question. (S. 11, pp. 10–11)

We must ask what it is that the British are trying to hide. As a consequence of the new vigor of Argentina's claims, among other factors, British authorities in the Foreign Office are beginning to question closely the legitimacy of the United Kingdom's title to the Malvinas. They had already decided at the beginning of 1900 to order a serious investigation into the historical background, entrusting this task to Gaston De Bernhardt, a librarian attached to the Foreign Office. Without passing judgment on Britain's title, in 1910 he produced a confidential memorandum on the merits of events, dating from the discovery of the islands through the time of his writing, which proved unexpectedly critical of the British position.

Since then, serious doubts arose in the British government concerning sovereign rights to the Malvinas Islands. These were stimulated further by a second document, which appeared in 1928 and ratified the earlier one. The doubts centered on historical and legal aspects and for a long time found their expression in an imperial policy of ignoring legitimate Argentine claims, because sovereignty over the islands was considered "not negotiable." (S. 21, p. 50)

I will prove, step by step, and by virtue of admissions by the British, how these uncertainties led them to put aside arguments based on discovery and effective occupation, the very events that, according to Lord Palmerston in his arrogant communication of 1833, legitimized the forcible expulsion of the small *criollo* garrison. The certainty, forged of a colonial vocation, which most British authorities, including officials of the Foreign Office, harbored during the nineteenth century, is crumbling. We will witness how the legal weakness of that line of argument led them later to put all their efforts into an interpretation of the events that transpired between 1811 (the year in which Spanish domination ended) and the usurpation of 1833, upon which to allege acquisitive prescription. Finally, we will see the advent of a new "rationale" which, without totally rejecting the influence of those decades, centers on the principle of self-determination, disingenuously articulated as a political axiom on which supposedly any solution must be based. A third Foreign Office memorandum, in 1946, confidential like the previous ones but made public by Peter Beck, demonstrates this tactical evolution and reveals how those doubts are consolidated into the "codification" of the British position on new grounds.

I want to chart that evolution to describe what I term the first "dilemma" facing the United Kingdom. This consists of the need to evaluate and choose arguments upon which to base the legitimacy of its juridical title to the Malvinas, naturally vis-à-vis the title of the Argentine Republic. I believe that this dilemma was resolved internally by successive British governments, but continues to be the Achilles heel of its current position. And it remains in effect since the way of the Law will always be open to the Argentine Republic, as long as it does not commit acts that imply a de jure recognition of the present de facto situation.

In my preface, I mentioned the detailed investigation that, at the request of Prime Minister Margaret Thatcher, Lord Franks completed with the object of elucidating possible government responsibility in not having predicted the Argentine occupation of April 2, 1982, in light of all the relevant factors of previous years. The harsh conclusion does not satisfy me because it should have set forth in detail the political responsibility of having neglected the mandate to negotiate the substance of the issue in good faith. Even so, I consider the January 1983 report an extraordinary contribution to a better understanding of the British attitude during the most dynamic period of bilateral negotiation with Argentina.

The United Kingdom's publication in an official document, discussed in Parliament, of the different proposals broached formally or off the record to Argentina during the period from 1965 to 1981—the document lists conditional transfer of sovereignty, condominium, Argentine sovereignty with a leaseback to the United Kingdom, and so forth—places any negotiating process on a new level of understanding. This approach, heretofore undisclosed, is definitively affirmed in the report drafted in 1983 and 1984 by a special committee of the House of Commons chaired by Sir Kershaw. In it, these options for resolution proposed in the past are evaluated and other alternatives are discussed, all directed toward a solution to the dispute over the sovereignty of the southern archipelagoes of the Malvinas, the South Georgias, and the South Sandwich Islands.

From the point of view of this essay, the lifting of the veil of confidentiality that protected the entire period—a laudable fact in itself—places the United Kingdom in a second dilemma. As clearly follows from the writings and opinions of its political and academic circles, this dilemma is how to ignore the recognition of Argentine rights over the southern archipelagoes implicit in the British proposals themselves. The second chapter proves that the dilemma is a double bind, devoid of favorable options for the Court of Saint James, just as former Prime Minister Margaret Thatcher understood it to be.

The possibility of arming the Malvinas militarily was an option that for years entered into the scenarios drawn up by the British authorities at different levels. The Franks Report reveals to us that this alternative has been around since at least the middle of the 1970s but also that it was rejected as inconvenient or impracticable. Because of circumstances known today, that option, called "Fortress Falklands," is a political and military reality.

Nonetheless, as I will prove in the third chapter, the highest levels of British government, political parties, and academia are every day more conscious that in the long run Fortress Falklands produces uncertainty, offers no guarantees of security, and does not comport with the potential for exploiting the natural resources of the region. On the contrary, those same circles today acknowledge that the armed conflict of 1982 did not resolve the dispute over sovereignty and that a stable and lasting solution to the Malvinas crisis must begin with an understanding with Argentina. This conviction is the source of what I term the third British dilemma: If Argentine involvement in the solution to the matter of the Malvinas is inevitable, how do they procure it while keeping in place all the interests at play?

The British admission that even today those "dilemmas" are present and that they must be overcome if one desires to come to a true solution to the dispute over sovereignty, leads us, as if by the hand, to the two final chapters. In the first, I approach, as a political analyst, the parameters that must be taken into account at the time of substantive negotiations on the institutional future of the Malvinas, the South Georgias, and the South Sandwich Islands. The elements that shape the Southwestern Atlantic scenario, with their conditioning and/or determining factors, just like their principal actors, are described in synthesized form but with sufficient clarity to make the conclusive reflections comprehensible. This goal requires that we enter into the complexities of the concept of sovereignty and the possibilities that would be available at the negotiating table. The reflections included as an epilogue to this essay are my personal opinions. On such a complex and politically sensitive subject no one is master of the truth, which in foreign affairs always depends on what is possible. Finally, the goal of the third section of the epilogue, the colophon, is not to lay out an alternative for solution to the sovereignty dispute with the United Kingdom, but to illustrate its multiple facets through possible options, constructed in light of what I understand are the vital interests in play.

I present the solution to the Malvinas question as a kind of jigsaw puzzle, a mosaic, the pieces of which must be assembled step by step, intelligently, tactfully, and patiently. And although I do not claim to suggest the pattern for the denouement of future negotiations, the reader will at least see that this essay outlines all the elements of the controversy, the first vital step toward solving the enigma.

1

The First British Dilemma: Overcoming the Weakness in Its Title to Sovereignty over the Malvinas

On January 8, 1834, one year after the small Argentine garrison was expelled from the islands by the British naval squadron commanded by Captain Onslow, Lord Palmerston, then British minister of foreign relations, finally responded to the Argentine protest, justifying the occupation of the Malvinas Islands in terms of the application of "British Sovereign Rights, which were founded upon original Discovery and the subsequent Occupation of those islands" (S. 21, p. 94).

In 1982, 150 years later and after a tragic armed conflict, Minister Francis Pym reiterated the legitimacy of British title to the islands, saying, "Our case rests on the facts, on prescription and on the principle of self-determination" (S. 21, p. 46).

The declaration of Lord Palmerston justifying seizure on the grounds of discovery and subsequent occupation, and the more recent declaration of the Foreign Office that British rights are founded in the first place on "the facts" makes it appropriate for us—in view of the ambiguity of the terminology used—to go back to the initial "facts" bearing on the question of title, beginning, although very briefly, with discovery.

As to the remaining sections of this chapter, their inclusion is necessary in any evaluation of the legitimacy of the rights of the parties in the sovereignty dispute under discussion. Although the base year is in my opinion 1811, when what is today the Argentine Republic inherited from the Spanish Crown its rights to sovereignty over the Malvinas Islands, the British government appears now to favor 1833 as the most significant year.

But in order for that to be, the most responsible British authors accept as the determining factor the establishment of whether by this date—that

7

of British usurpation—there was a legitimate holder of sovereignty over the islands. Consequently, they also recognize the necessity of delving into the historical facts at least until the eighteenth century, when the first acts of effective occupation occurred.

In summary, since its original expression in the note of Lord Palmerston until what today would represent his preferences, the British position in relation to the best title over the southern archipelagoes has been based on four arguments. In order not to exclude any, I devote to them this entire chapter.

DISCOVERY

I will discuss discovery only briefly because, in spite of Lord Palmerston's declaration, it is not difficult to demonstrate, even using British sources, that the Malvinas were not discovered by Great Britain. I want to point out that, in addition to works by British writers, I quote in this first chapter from the only work in the English language that has researched with exceptional detail and seriousness the historical and diplomatic events relevant to the Malvinas Islands, until the piracy of 1833. This source, by a U.S., not British, author, is Julius Goebel's book *The Struggle for the Falkland Islands* (S. 8)—published by Yale University in 1927—which has even been used as a reference by the Foreign Office itself.

In probing the historical basis for Argentina's rights, I find they are rooted in and derive from those of Spain. So if it is a question of comparing title, it is the Spanish Crown's that would have to be juxtaposed with the British Crown's.

Spain's title predates the discovery and goes back to the Papal Bull of 1493, based on what has been called the concept of "adjudication" resulting from the recognition of the temporal power of the popes. As to the discovery itself, one should remember Amerigo Vespucci, who might have first sighted the Malvinas Islands in 1502 during his third voyage, as Goebel mentions, quoting the Frenchman Bougainville.

If Goebel, after commenting upon the opinions of geographers of the period, is not totally insistent as to discovery by the Florentine navigator in the name of the King of Spain, he is even less so with respect to discovery by the English navigators Davis and Hawkins, upon which Lord Palmerston's declaration must be based in order to be valid. Goebel points out that claims based on the voyages of these two English navigators are poorly substantiated, and that Hawkins may have been on the Patagonian coast, not in the islands at all.

Peter Beck echoes Goebel's assessments and moreover comments that the British government's support for Hawkins and Davis "has been qualified by private admission relating to the imprecise and confused nature of the evidence." He summarizes: "As a result, the facts of discovery, such as they are, do little to the British claim." And he immediately wonders whether it is even of any interest at all, given that "discovery, unless followed within a reasonable period of time by effective occupation, confers no legal title." (S. 21, pp. 37–38) In his last sentence Beck introduces a new fact that is worth exploring: It is no longer important who made the discovery, but whether the event is relevant in and of itself.

Here it is appropriate to quote the opinion of the British researcher J. Myhre of the Department of International Relations of the London School of Economics, who, in commenting on the judgment of Max Huber in the case of the Palmas Islands, says: "Discovery, then, confers on a state an inchoate title. That is to say, discovery does give right to an exclusive right to occupy the area. Unless the right is exercised, though, no firm title exists" (S. 18, p. 26).

Beck recognizes that "during the eighteenth and nineteenth centuries prior discovery figured prominently in British historical and legal rationales for title to the islands, but during the present century this aspect has been toned down, even pushed aside, in the light of an appreciation of the obscure and uncertain nature of the evidence" (S. 21, p. 38; Peter Beck, *The Falkland Islands and Dependencies,* COI, London, 1982).

The British authors quoted imply, on one hand, that discovery alone is not enough to confer title and, on the other, that it is moreover uncertain whether the discovery of the Malvinas was by Great Britain. Beck thinks the discoverer was really Sebald de Weert, who was Dutch.

To seal these commentaries from British sources, a memorandum drawn up by the Foreign Office on December 17, 1982 (127/82–83/FM), in response to the Kershaw Committee, concludes that as to the original British discovery, the evidence is "obscure and uncertain. Our claim to first discovery has never of itself formed the basis for our claim to sovereignty over the islands" (S. 2, p. 144).

Within this change of course, from the confidence of Lord Palmerston in the note with which he claims to whitewash the usurpation of 1833, to the current doubts in the Foreign Office, Beck leans toward the latter, and as to the value of discovery, he says that it is not really of any legal importance (S. 21 p. 38). If the Foreign Office says that its position is based on the "facts" one has to go back to the eighteenth century—to the first occupation—because of its importance to 1833.

If British writers pose this challenge, it is not our intention to avoid it, but as far as discovery is concerned, what is clear from the one party's own admission is that it was not by Great Britain nor does it have any significance in the rights it asserts over the Malvinas.

EFFECTIVE OCCUPATION

Respect for international law in the eighteenth century:
The cancellation of a British expedition.

I have made clear that the British have backed away from the argument of discovery per se and are emphasizing subsequent effective occupation. I share Peter Beck's opinion on the importance of the events that transpired in the islands in the eighteenth century, that is, the raising of two settlements in the Malvinas, to a legal evaluation of the occurrences of 1833, which in his opinion is the base year for any claim to title over the islands.

But first, a general observation is in order. The first effective occupation in the Malvinas Islands occurred at a particular time in history when the great European powers of the period determined the public law in force for a world with Europe as its epicenter. From an era characterized by wars, alliances, and counteralliances, we must examine some of the international agreements that impact on this discussion.

The first is the Treaty of Peace and Friendship between Great Britain and Spain signed in Utrecht on July 13, 1713, which in the final part of Point VIII reestablishes the possessions of the Spanish Crown in the so-called West Indies. Among these possessions were the islands and territories of the southern seas, in which are located the three archipelagoes of the Anglo-Argentine dispute.

With respect to this convention, and also as immediate background to our subject, one must refer to the Treaty of Paris, which ended the Seven Years War. This, in keeping with previous peace agreements, revalidated and confirmed the whole series of treaties signed from Westphalia to the Treaty of Madrid of 1950. Goebel maintains that "the whole system of public law previous to the war was confirmed for Europe and America, except as it was modified in the new arrangement" (S. 8, pp. 209–216). In this way the Treaty of Utrecht was ratified as in force and would be invoked by Spain upon the British trespass in the Malvinas Islands.

The aborted British expedition of 1748 stands in eloquent testimony to the value and interpretation that Great Britain gave its commitments to Spain with respect to the recognition of Spain's exclusive dominion in the southern seas. Samuel Johnson, the English author of a well-known, officially commissioned pamphlet, said that after the voyages of Anson were made public, interest in the lands of the southern seas grew, and in 1748 several ships were made ready in this connection. However, when the plans were finalized, the British ambassador in Madrid, Benjamin Keen, had to clarify that the purpose was only to discover new territory and not to settle it. Even so, the Admiralty decided to abandon its original plan and not to undertake new discoveries. There seemed little rationale in "going so far only to come back," and finally "the Ministry dismissed the whole design" (S. 7 pp. 12–13).

Johnson concluded that after this episode, the islands were "forgotten or neglected" until the designation of the Earl of Egmont to direct naval affairs, who decided to send an expedition to the islands under the command of Captain Byron.

The two settlements.

Beck agrees with Deas and notes that nothing in particular happened with respect to the islands until the end of the Seven Years War (1763), when almost immediately two parallel events occurred (S. 21, p. 38).

It is uncontested that the first settlement in the Malvinas Islands owed its existence to the Frenchman Antoine Louis de Bougainville, who obtained authorization from the French Crown to send an expedition to the islands at his own expense.

On January 31, 1764, West Falkland was sighted, but seeking a more favorable place to anchor, the expedition moved toward East Falkland, entering what we now know as Berkeley Sound. Goebel says that on March 17 the site upon which to raise the settlement was selected "and a fort, St. Louis, was erected, together with several huts. Formal possession in the name of Louis XV was taken of all the islands on April 5, 1764, giving them the name of Les Malouines" (S. 8, p. 226).

In the same year, 1764, the British government, according to Beck, "unaware of the French occupation on East Falkland, sent an expedition under Captain John Byron" (S. 21, pp. 38–39). He arrived in the Saunders Islands of the Western Malvinas on January 12, 1765, and christened a natural harbor Port Egmont, in honor of the First Lord of the Admiralty.

Although of no importance whatsoever to the question of title, it should be noted here that serious doubts exist as to Byron's supposed possessory actions, as the 1947 annual report from the Colonial Office points out.

On June 21, Byron returned to England and submitted a report on his voyage to Henry Conway, British secretary of state for the Southern Department, prompting him to request the Admiralty to send a new expedition to the islands. Bougainville's settlement was by then public knowledge, and in his note reporting on the voyage, Conway was unequivocal in saying that anyone found to be in the islands illegally would be compelled to leave or to submit to the Crown of Great Britain. (S. 8, pp. 234–235)

Complying with these instructions, Captain John McBride, in command of the HMS *Jason,* weighed anchor for the islands, arriving at Port Egmont on January 8, 1766, almost two years after the French landing on Isla Soledad and 14 months after Spain had taken possession (Goebel, op. cit., p. 238).

A harsh winter led to the postponement of further investigation of any other presence in the islands, but on December 2, 1766, McBride finally discovered the French settlement. He sent a note to the governor, Monsieur de Neville, asking by whose authority it had been erected, and received a firm response that, since his arrival was hostile, he would be considered an aggressor. Finally McBride, after warning the French that they should leave the settlement, departed for Port Egmont and in January 1767 returned to England.

Regarding this episode, Goebel states without circumlocution: "There can be no question that under the existing state of public law McBride's proceeding was highly irregular" (S. 8, p. 240). Meanwhile, the Spanish government, which had learned of Bougainville's settlement at Port Louis, vigorously protested to the French government.

In answer to those who from time to time point to the paltry value of these rocky islands, let the record reflect that already by the middle of the eighteenth century the three most important European powers were asserting their rights over the Malvinas, and as we shall see, they were very close to entering into a costly military confrontation in order to possess them.

Spain takes control of the Malvinas.
The forced abandonment of the British
settlement and the political crisis.

Carlos III's protest to Louis XV led to diplomatic negotiations between the two courts united by the Family Pact. As a consequence, Port Louis was handed over to the Spanish Crown in April of 1767, a concession based on the application of international agreements in force, especially the Treaty of Utrecht.

Beck comments on this political-diplomatic episode by saying that given the pressure from the Spanish Crown and the close Franco-Spanish dynastic relations, and by virtue of 618,108 pounds sterling in monetary compensation, agreement was reached on October 4, 1766, "for the surrender of Port Louis. The formal transfer of Bougainville's settlement was performed in April, 1767, when Port Louis was re-named Puerto Soledad. Already in October 1766, the islands had been incorporated into the jurisdiction of the Captaincy General of Buenos Aires, and Don Felipe Ruiz Puente became the first Governor of the Malvinas" (S. 21, p. 64).

It is interesting to quote the memorandum on this particular detail, one that Malcolm Deas brought to the attention of the House of Commons. Deas emphasizes, as does Beck, that France, in relinquishing the Bougainville settlement, conceded its illegality.

With the islands already under the control of the Spanish Crown and with the continent aware of the existence of a British garrison in the Saunders

Islands, an order was sent on February 25, 1768, to Bucarelli, the captain general of Buenos Aires. This left no doubt as to the will of Carlos III regarding the Malvinas. It said, "No English establishments are to be permitted and, you are to expel by force any already set up if they do not obey the warnings, in conformity with the law" (S. 8, p. 271).

In the interim, some rather unfriendly contacts had taken place between Captain Hunt, in charge of Port Egmont, and Ruiz Puente, governor of what was now called Puerto Soledad. The latter had insinuated in diplomatic terms that British presence in Port Egmont "must be accidental, as the contrary would be in absolute violation of the treaties in effect and in bad faith." Hunt did not hesitate to respond in a belligerent tone, confirming that the islands belonged to the British Crown under whose orders he threatened, "I warn you to leave the said islands," and he gave Ruiz Puente six months in which to do so. (Ibid., p. 274)

Meanwhile, Bucarelli had taken all the necessary steps to prepare an expedition capable of subjugating the British settlement. On June 4, 1770, after several skirmishes and shots, Port Egmont had to surrender. The British garrison was given 20 days to leave.

In less than four years, Carlos III had reacted with a firm hand and had liberated the Malvinas from both "intruders," as the North American Richard Perl terms the French and British who occupied the islands.

Deas also used the term intruders with respect to the British settlement when he stated before the Kershaw Committee: "The French conceded they had no right to be there and conceded . . . their settlement to Spain. Our settlement was, I think, intrusive. It was against the provisions of the Treaty of Utrecht" (S. 2, p. 132).

The expulsion of the British from Port Egmont was to lead to one of the major political and diplomatic crises of the century between England and the two Crowns united by the Family Pact. War seemed inevitable.

Masserano's declaration.
The secret promise.
The Convention of Nootka Sound.

Whether because of the estrangement between the French court and Choiseul, who had become entangled as mediator in the Anglo-Spanish conflict, or for other reasons, in January, Spain's position became more flexible and the British representative, Harris, who had been "summoned" from his post in Madrid, received instructions to remain. On January 22, 1771, Masserano formulated his well-known declaration that contained the promise to return Port Egmont. The last paragraph, however, included a reservation of rights that takes on enormous significance in the litigation over title to the Malvinas. It read as follows:

> The Prince of Masserano declares at the same time in the name of His Master that the commitment of His Catholic Majesty to return to His British Majesty the possession of the port called Egmont cannot nor must affect in any way the question of the prior right of sovereignty over the Malouines Islands, also known as Falkland. (S. 25, p. 36)

This declaration prompted a response from the earl of Rochford in terms that, in relevant part, amounted to an acceptance of the contents of Masserano's pronouncement, without any exceptions. Especially clear is the reservation of rights of sovereignty formulated by Spain. Had that not been acceptable, the declaration would have been rejected. In one of his works on the subject, Bonifacio del Carril maintains that in the official edition of the State Papers of 1771, which he has seen, the original title of the British response was "acceptance" and not "counter declaration" as is generally thought (S. 24, p. 52).

The British writer Jeffrey D. Myhre confirms the value of this "exchange of notes," saying,

> The contents of those agreements are quite legally binding. Spain did return Port Egmont to Britain, but it was not returning British sovereignty with it, supposing Port Egmont was ever under British sovereignty. The port was to be a British base in Spanish territory. The British declaration did not dispute the Spanish reservation of sovereignty and it must be interpreted as recognition of Spanish sovereignty over the islands. (S. 18, p. 32)

Regarding the interpretation of this exchange of notes, Samuel Johnson himself, who wrote his pamphlet in 1771 in the heat of the moment, concluded:

> We therefore called for restitution, not as a confession of right, but as a reparation of honour, which required that we should be restored to our former state upon the island, and that the King of Spain should disavow the action of his Governor. (S. 7, p. 36)

He adds that, from all appearances, the Spanish desired compensation for Hunt's insulting attitude, which they never got.

No one has researched this fascinating period in European history without linking the restitution of Port Egmont to the British Crown to an eventual secret promise to abandon the settlement within a short period of time. To those wishing to explore this further, I recommend Goebel's book, which devotes nearly a hundred pages to the subject.

As to the facts, one should mention briefly that the restitution of Port Egmont took place on September 15, 1771, after laborious diplomatic negotiations—with the participation of France, which was always active on the European chessboard of the period.

Acknowledging the existence and the effectiveness of a secret promise, the United Kingdom abandoned the settlement on May 20, 1774, only 32 months later. It is of little importance that the British fastened to the fort a lead plaque with an inscription reaffirming British rights, or that they left their flag raised.

Of course, there remained no certainty that the evacuation was the result of, or was connected to, a prior commitment. Instead, economic reasons were given and testimony inconsistent with the existence of a secret promise. Certainly the British abandonment of the Malvinas occurred in a relatively short period of time, which satisfied the Spanish Crown and left no reason to continue discussing peripheral matters. This became even more the case when, a few years later, what remained of the British settlement was ordered destroyed, which it was in 1780, without any reaction from the owner of the plaque and the flag.

With respect to the secret British commitment to abandon Port Egmont, Beck says that this "thesis" was "encouraged by a dispatch dated 14 February 1771 from the British Ambassador in Madrid, who mentioned the Spanish government's report saying: 'We have given a verbal assurance to evacuate Falkland's Island in the space of two months'" (S. 21, p. 40). Goebel concludes: "England finally executed the promises by which the declaration [of 1771] had been induced. . . . We are justified in dismissing as a mere diplomatic phrase the reference to a policy of economy" (S. 8, p. 343).

Deas, too, stated to the Kershaw Committee: "I think it is pretty clear that there was a tacit agreement that we were going to stay there a bit to save face and then to withdraw" (S. 2, p. 133).

In spite of this firm and consistent opinion on the existence of a secret promise, the Foreign Office in a memorandum dated December 17, 1983, to the Kershaw Committee said: "There is no record of any written agreement or of any formal commitment by Britain to renounce sovereignty or withdrawal from Port Egmont" (S. 2, p. 144, question 3). Certainly there was not, because it was a secret promise. It does not appear that the response cited can alter the express opinions of British writers who, like those quoted, are mostly inclined toward the existence of such a promise. In this, as in other matters, I prefer to let the reader judge whether a confession by the one party exists or not.

As for other British arguments such as the one having to do with the plaque that was left behind reaffirming British rights, let us see what Professor Deas thinks of them:

> We talked of economy and left a plaque, but on balance I would conclude that we had little or no intention of returning. We showed no renewed interest in the islands before the late 1820s. We ignored the demolition of the abandoned settlement, signed the Nootka Sound Convention (1790) renouncing future establishments on "eastern and western coasts of South America and the islands adjacent." (Ibid., p. 128)

And as for the agreement of 1771, he adds, "It certainly goes no further than to restore to us Port Egmont" (Ibid., p. 133). Finally, summarizing his point of view, he affirms, "We established a toe-hold, but not an exclusive one, and then let go" (Ibid., p. 128).

Other British writers have downplayed the importance of the plaque. Beck, for example, also picks up a semantic point from the plaque of 1774, pointing out that it refers to the "Falkland Island," in the singular, and that it "was employed to limit the British claim to Port Egmont" (S. 25, p. 65). "While in the eyes of many international jurists, the plaque of 1774 would prove incapable of preserving the British claim over a period of 59 years" (S. 11, p. 19).

Another piece of evidence that is very favorable to the Argentine case in the Malvinas is the signing, after these events, of the Convention of Nootka Sound of 1790, mentioned by Deas as of great importance.

It states that, with relation to the east and west coasts of South America and the adjacent islands, Great Britain "shall not erect in the future any settlement on the coast . . . and the adjacent islands occupied by Spain," and allow for only temporary structures in support of fishing activities. This is to say that, while the doctrine of "closed seas" had been abrogated in favor of the Spanish Crown and of the entire system of treaties on which the Spanish colonial system was based, British rights to colonize were limited to the northwest coast of North America. (S. 8, p. 429)

Goebel says that this agreement is very significant in the legal status of the Malvinas, since, in a solemn treaty, the British now had admitted the de facto occupation of the Malvinas group "not to be an occupation in the legal sense." This means that in exchange for the acknowledgment of English navigation and fishing rights, Spain was assured recognition of its sovereignty of the already occupied territories. (S. 8, p. 430) Deas too states that Spain was considered sovereign in the adjacent islands according to the convention and that under it, Great Britain was granted many things in exchange for what it had relinquished, leading to the belief that "there was good diplomatic reason . . . for not putting the Falklands into it even if we had had a mind to" (S. 2, p. 135).

Summarizing the above observations by British writers, all of them confirm that in 1811, when it abandoned the southern archipelagoes as a consequence of the loss of its colonies in the Americas, Spain's title was indisputably superior to any held by the British. By that date, Great Britain having been an intruder for a few years on one of the smaller islands, had then abandoned it, probably because of an understanding with its legitimate owner—the Spanish Crown—and did not object to the total destruction of the settlement nor to 37 years of Spanish occupation of the region as provided in an international treaty specifically designed to readjust the dominion and zones of influence of the great powers of that era.

Abandoned by Spain, the archipelagoes
fall under Argentine sovereignty.

As a consequence of the revolution of May 1810 in Argentina and of the election of the First Junta in Buenos Aires, on January 8, 1811, it was resolved that colonial dominion in the islands must cease, and from Montevideo the Spanish government ordered the evacuation of the settlement at Puerto Soledad.

Meanwhile, after the Congress of Vienna of 1815, which had put an end to the domination of Spain by the Bonaparte family and had restored the Bourbons in Madrid, the independence movement of what is now Argentina was consolidated in the Congress of Tucumán of 1816, and on July 9 of that year, the United Provinces of the River Plate were declared independent from the Spanish Crown.

These events, full of historical significance, also take on great importance in the legal dispute over the Malvinas Islands. Indeed, the Spanish abandonment in 1811 and the legal principle of the Succession of States led to new lines of contention between the two parties disputing the sovereignty of the southern archipelagoes.

The British line of argument—which is incongruent with the principles invoked by Argentina—is based on the following:

i. Spanish abandonment returned the islands to the status of *terra nullius,* that is, a land belonging to no one.
ii. Recognition of the Succession of States in favor of Argentina is based on the principle of *uti possidetis jure,* which lacks universal validity and is only applied among Latin American countries to their own continent.
iii. The actions of the United Provinces of the River Plate from 1820 onward were insufficient to establish its claim of sovereignty.

It is appropriate to analyze what opinion the official arguments merit among other British writers, in order to determine if here also lies another "confession" as to lack of consistency.

The first two points are interrelated and we will analyze them in this section. The third will be analyzed in the next section.

The terra nullius argument. To begin with, Malcolm Deas says, "Yes, but the gap is essentially 1811–1820 . . . a territory does not become res nullius as soon as it is abandoned by those who claim to own it" (S. 2, p. 132). And he insists that just because the Argentines did not immediately take possession of all the territory they had inherited from Spain did not mean that it was "up for grabs . . . and territory claimable by any nation that had a mind to" (Ibid., pp. 134–135).

The principle of "uti possidetis jure." On this question we can quote J. Myhre, who, in the work cited above, maintains: "This principle, uti possidetis, is a customary Latin American law that defines the boundaries of Latin American states as those which prevailed over the territory when it was Spanish" (S. 18, p. 27). That is, he accepts it as a generally practiced Latin American law, and he adds:

> As for the accusation that uti possidetis is a regional principle . . . , this simply is not true. It must be observed that . . . it can only be relevant where decolonization has occurred. . . . It is hard to see how the contention that it is only a regional practice can be made in light of the facts. In those parts of the world where it has any relevance, i.e., in former colonial possessions, . . . it is universal state practice.

He cites cases in Africa and Asia and concludes, "Whether it is called uti possidetis or not, the existence of the principle cannot be denied." (Ibid., p. 33)

Another British writer, Denzil Dunnett, also subscribes to its universal validity in the context of decolonization noting "a historic resolution of the Organization for African Unity at its first Assembly in Cairo in July 1964 . . . affirming the maintenance of African frontiers as of the date of independence" (S. 10, p. 417).

As if this range of opinions favorable to Argentina's thesis were not enough, it was none other than Lord Kershaw who recalled the case of Zimbabwe's independence from the United Kingdom and said that, with respect to its borders, the territory over which the United Kingdom had exercised sovereignty "was inherited by the new government of Zimbabwe" (S. 4, p. 120).

An internationalist of the stature of M. Akehurst, professor of law at the University of Keele, conclusively stated in a document on the Malvinas Islands:

> Argentina succeeded to Spain's title. It is a rule of international law that a newly independent State which was formerly a colony succeeds to all the territory within the former colonial boundaries. This rule, known to Latin American lawyers as the principle of uti possidetis, is not peculiar to Latin America; it has also been applied to former colonies in Africa and Asia. (S. 25, p. 130)

In any event, for those who continue to try to deny the principle of uti possidetis or its validity outside the American continent, Myhre maintains that "if uti possidetis did not apply, then the islands became terra nullis and the Argentine occupation of 1820 was completely legal" (S. 18, p. 33).

When the Commission of the House of Commons asked whether there were any doubts that "the Falklands prior to 1820 or in 1820 were a Spanish possession in that part of the world," Malcolm Deas answered, "I do not think there can be" (S. 2, p. 135). And he adds that strong arguments exist for saying that the authority in that part of the world that was inherited from the Spanish empire is also heir to the Falklands (S. 2, p. 135).

It is not surprising that Fitzmaurice himself, who was for many years legal adviser of the Foreign Office, declared in 1936: "Our case has certain weaknesses mainly on account of doubts over whether the islands were res nullius at the time of Britain's initial claim in 1833" (S. 9, p. 53).

If the legal adviser to the Foreign Office himself has such serious doubts, what more remains to be said, given the opinions of distinguished British specialists, many of whom, such as Deas and Beck, were called before the Foreign Affairs Committee of the House of Commons to testify on the subject because of their acknowledged expertise and professional competence.

I have no doubt; I understand that British arguments (i) and (ii) as described above have been demolished by that party's own admissions.

Argentine acts of sovereignty. Protests by the United Kingdom.

We recall that the third element in the British argument, under (iii) above, terms as insufficient the legal acts undertaken by Argentina between 1820 and 1833 to alter the islands' alleged status as *terra nullius*. We have seen that this alleged status is a fallacy, but we do not want to avoid analyzing this last point.

The activity undertaken by the new state is quite remarkable if one bears in mind that it obviously had other priorities during its first years of independence. Not even five years had passed since its declaration of independence when possessory actions were initiated in 1820.

I am not speaking of any British activity, because it is well settled that "after 1774 Britain's interest in the islands was effectively suspended until 19 November 1829" when a protest note was lodged (S. 21, p. 42).

I could dedicate several pages to Argentine documentary sources on this period, but this is not my purpose nor my method. I prefer instead to give the floor to Malcolm Deas, who in the above-cited memorandum begins by granting little importance to whether the islands were abandoned between 1811 and 1820, since, in any event, "nobody claimed them" (S. 2, p. 128, point iii). Called upon to explain the point more fully, he said that in 1820 the successor to Spain was the United Provinces of the River Plate, and he enumerated its legal actions to take possession of the islands: "It gets going again in the person of Colonel Jewett who was the Province's naval officer who went there and formally claimed the islands for the United Provinces of the River Plate." And Deas continues that this was effected with a declaration to the whalers present, letting them know "that the United Provinces was back in action and was formally reclaiming these islands." That declaration was made before 50 whaling captains and there is evidence that this "statement got around." (S. 2, p. 132) In any event, there is no room for any doubt that it was received in the United Kingdom from the mouth of Captain Weddell, that pioneer of the Antarctic seas. On November 6, the formal act of possession of the islands on the part of the United Provinces took place.

Regarding these possessory actions, Goebel recalls that they were followed by others, "to secure the sovereignty over the islands and to promote a successful colony." He cites the designation of Don Pablo Aregusti as governor in 1823 and the Confederation's grant of concessions on Isla Soledad (East Falkland) to Jorge Pacheco and Luis Vernet, including the lands, use of cattle, and fishing rights. Then he mentions Robert Schofield's expedition and the settlement erected in 1824, which was abandoned the following year, a failure that did not discourage Luis Vernet who in January of 1826 left for the islands, where he finally was able to raise a settlement. (S. 8, pp. 434–435)

Returning to Akehurst's memorandum, Goebel states:

> Argentina established a settlement in the East Falkland in the 1820s, and this settlement remained until the settlers were evicted by the UK in 1833. So, even if Spain's title to East Falkland lapsed in 1811, with the result that East Falkland became terra nullus again, Argentina could claim that she had acquired sovereignty over East Falkland by occupation, by establishing her own effective control over East Falkland. (S. 25, p. 131)

Deas also refers to what he says international law terms "state actions": activities of the type the experts in international law and the British authorities themselves cite in other contexts as "adequate state activity" including in the Dependencies, meaning the South Georgia and South Sandwich islands (S. 2, p. 132).

In reality it would be very difficult, even for an Argentine writer, to write anything more convincing than these candid British authors have written as to the undeniable legitimacy of the title that Argentina retained over the Malvinas in January 1833, when by an act of piracy, which occurred rather frequently in those days, for the second time in the history of the islands Great Britain became an intruder.

We see that the United Provinces took the necessary steps to exercise fully their sovereign rights in the Malvinas. The islands were occupied by an Argentine colony and garrison at the time the British arrived and were a part of the United Provinces.

The exercise of jurisdiction in fishing matters.
The episode of vandalism involving the USS Lexington.

The preservation and control of fisheries was an immediate concern of the new government, which was determined to exclude third parties who would not submit to payment of a licensing fee fixed at six dollars a ton by a decree of October 22, 1821. Vernet, with a base in the islands, applied for and obtained in January 1828 exclusive fishing rights for the colony. On June 10, 1829, a new decree created a Civil and Military Command under a governor with headquarters on Isla Soledad (East Falkland) and jurisdiction over the Malvinas and the adjacent islands all the way to Cape Horn. Vernet was designated governor, becoming thus an official of the new Republic "with the obligation of enforcing its laws" (S. 8, pp. 436–437). It is this designation that prompted a protest note, the first sign of any British reaction after more than half a century of silence.

It should be emphasized that the possessory actions referred to above were being carried out in 1823, when the United Kingdom recognized the United Provinces as a sovereign state, and in 1825, when both countries signed the Treaty of Peace and Friendship, without any protest or reference to the islands on the part of the British.

Nor did the British protest note of 1829 even satisfy the British prime minister, the Duke of Wellington, who at that time, in June 1829, wrote, "It is not at all clear to me that we have ever possessed the sovereignty of these islands" (correspondence and memoranda of the Duke of Wellington, vol. 6, John Murray, 1877, p. 41).

This paragraph, quoted by Beck, is in the response of the Duke of Wellington to a letter from John Murray, who was then acting as "private secretary of state." In Murray's letter, dated July 23, 1829, he suggests some interest in constructing a British settlement in the Malvinas. In his statement in the House of Commons, Malcolm Deas quoted the content of Murray's letter. His simple reading demonstrates British expedience in taking advantage of the situation: "The interval between the cessation of the power of old Spain and the consolidation of that of the new government of South America would be the best time for our resuming our former possession of the Falkland Islands" (S. 2, p. 133).

With respect to this British protest, Deas concludes that there is "a lot of doubt about whether we were in the right doing that." He adds that as time passed with nothing being done, people will say that our "claim lapsed," especially in view of the Nootka Sound Convention, "which," Deas points out, "we were using at that time in other parts of the world." Deas concludes by asking: "Does that make it clear?" (Ibid., p. 133)

For me it is very clear and I am sure that it is clear to the reader too.

But events were to move rapidly. Vernet's efforts to implement his directives in fishing matters met head on with the constant havoc wreaked by sealers. On July 30, 1831, he proceeded to apprehend three U.S. vessels that in spite of prior warnings had continued to violate the regulations in force.

This action by Vernet prompted aggressive communications to Foreign Minister Anchorena from George W. Slacum, the imprudent U.S. consular officer in Buenos Aires. Apparently without instructions from his government, but probably incited by the British consul general, Woodbine Parish, to whose pen the strange protest of 1829 is attributed, Slacum convinced Commander Silas Duncan, commander of the schooner USS *Lexington,* who occasionally visited the port of Buenos Aires, to come to the protection of U.S. citizens. Duncan sailed to the islands, entering the Bay of Puerto Soledad on December 28, 1831. After an action more appropriate for a buccaneer than for a commander of a warship, he entered the port under the French flag, invited two of Vernet's lieutenants on board, and then took them prisoner. He then landed, seized weapons and seal skins, destroyed gunpowder, sacked living quarters, arrested almost the entire population, and, finally, left, declaring the islands "free of all governments."

I have briefly related the facts, but as always what is important to me in this essay is the evaluation of the facts by the British. Let us listen to what Malcolm Deas says of this brutal occurrence, which is probably at the root of the piracy of 1833: "The destruction of the Argentine settlement by the USS *Lexington* in December 1831, with some connivance from the British consul in Buenos Aires, was a highly improper act, which did not make the islands 'free of all government'" (S. 2, p. 128).

Perhaps with a certain black humor Deas places the apprehending of the U.S. fishermen in the context of acts of sovereignty by the Argentine government and adds, "They get into trouble with the Americans, with the United States by being over-active, if you like" (Ibid., p. 132). Noting the devastating action by the *Lexington,* he says, "I would say that is a main reason why the islands were a bit of a shambles in 1833." And he concludes, "The Buenos Aires government was in the process of reestablishing its authority in the islands when the HMS Clio arrived and expelled its agents in January 1833." (Ibid., p. 135)

This obvious nexus between the brigandage of the *Lexington* and the later British piracy in 1833 was also implicit in the report of the parliamentary committee chaired by Sir Kershaw.

In any event, with respect to the ignominious act of aggression by the USS *Lexington* and the strange declaration of its commander, a memorandum from the Foreign Office dated December 17, 1982, acknowledged that "Captain Duncan's action . . . would not have been sufficient to establish terra nullius status" (S. 2, p. 146, paragraph 8).

British usurpation by force in 1833.

Obviously the action of the USS *Lexington* and the behavior of Consul Slacum strained Argentine-U.S. relations. Official contacts with the diplomat were suspended. Francis Baylies, a lawyer from Massachusetts, was appointed chargé d'affaires in Buenos Aires, and he arrived at his post in June 1832. Due to the failure of his attempts to negotiate fishing rights, his tour would last only three months.

Before leaving, Baylies met with the British minister and told him that the United States had no claim to the Malvinas except for fishing rights, but given that the United Kingdom had asserted "her sovereignty right to the Falklands, this would not justify her countenancing a horde of pirates on the islands for the purpose of annoying American commerce." The minister answered that because Argentina had sent the schooner *Sarandí* to the islands, "he assumed that Great Britain would take action." (S. 8, p. 454)

The United States, in other words, was already intervening in the Malvinas question, clearly showing its preferences as to who should exercise control over the islands.

The preceding is relevant as immediate background to demonstrate the British government's true strategy in sending warships to the Malvinas. The HMS *Clio,* commanded by Captain Onslow, arrived in the islands on December 20, 1832. After trying to repair the old fortress on Saunders Island, he headed for Puerto Soledad arriving on January 2, 1833. There he found anchored the *Sarandí,* an armed schooner under the command of José María Pinedo, who had brought the new governor, Juan Esteban Mertimer, to the islands. The latter died in an insurrection that Pinedo had managed to put down.

Onslow told him that he had come to take possession in the name of His British Majesty, and he sent Pinedo a note indicating that the following day he would exercise his sovereign rights and would raise the British flag. He asked that the Argentine colors be lowered.

It is important to relate how the Argentine eviction took place given that in large measure the legality of the disputed title to sovereignty over the islands lies in the alleged legitimacy of the action by the United Kingdom. As in other cases, I will rely on irreproachable British sources and on a work by a U.S. researcher, Julius Goebel, the historical merit of which is unimpeachable. Goebel describes what happened in this manner:

> Pinedo at once waited upon Onslow, uttering vain protest against the outrage. He declared roundly he would never lower the Argentine flag. The

next morning, however, a force was landed, the British flag was raised, the Argentine ensign was struck and subsequently delivered to the *Sarandí.*" (S. 8., pp. 455–456)

It is clear; there was no armed Argentine resistance—Pinedo had no troops to offer any—but there was no surrender either, not even of the Argentine colors. This version coincides totally with Captain Onslow's own report exactly as revealed in the December 17, 1982, memorandum of the Foreign Office, and it is ironic, if not a cruel joke, that in the same document the British Foreign Office states that "the Falkland Islands were not taken by force." Commander Pinedo and members of the garrison were "persuaded to leave peacefully." (S. 2, p. 146, question 9)

Professor emeritus of the University of London and for nine years president of the European Commission on Human Rights, James Fawcett, could hardly be branded as favoring the Argentine side. Nonetheless, he rejects the theory of "persuasion" and acknowledges an act of force. In his opinion, however, it did not weaken the superior British claim, because at the time, force was not contrary to international law.

And Fawcett adds that it is difficult for the Argentines to understand why their forcible occupation of April 1982, which some consider comparable, is illegal if the occupation of 1833 was legal. He concludes that the obligation incorporated later in the United Nations Charter resulted in a different standard.

What is certain is that the British position presents many contradictions and reversals, which become only more accentuated with the passage of time.

According to Beck, when asked by the Kershaw Committee, the key issue is that the United Kingdom took control of the islands, founding its claim not on a right of conquest, as Fawcett suggests, but "in fact claiming that she was re-asserting her ancient rights and this was the basic British rationale used when she took control of the islands in 1833" (S. 4, p. 119). Obviously he was right, as were those questioning him when they concluded, "But if she had not got any ancient rights she could not re-assert them, but she physically occupied with force" (Ibid.).

Added to this host of pronouncements favorable to the Argentine cause is that of Jeffrey Myhre, who states that, given it is already almost undeniable that Argentina held title in 1833, "then . . . the British invasion cannot be anything but an illegal act of aggression" (S. 18, p. 33).

Malcolm Deas, when asked how Latin America sees this historical argument, answers: "The historical argument of Latin America on these events is bound to be that Great Britain, the leading naval power of the time, somewhat deviously took advantage of a weak emerging nation" (S. 2, p. 129). And he adds, "Our legal case in 1833 seems to me very much rather cobbled together and not altogether sincere" (Ibid., p. 136).

In one of his works, Beck brings up an interesting change of phrase demonstrating the true nature of the act of January 1833. The words "annexed them by force in 1833" were replaced in the original version of an official British encyclopedia by the charming phrase "took the opportunity of occupying the islands."

In closing this section I would point to another episode, almost as comical, which, although it appears a digression, helps one understand the mentality of the era. The memorandum of the Foreign Office dated December 17, 1982, referring to the English invasions of Buenos Aires in 1806—there are no doubts that the British were active at the time and had the area in their imperial view—says that Commander Sir Home Popham "not having immediate work to do, had decided on his own, without any government authorization, to take an expedition to South America" (S. 2, p. 144).

There is no doubt as to the dangerous nature of British naval personnel of the time, whether their actions were official or resulted from idleness.

Partial assessment with the aid of the Foreign Office.

I am convinced at this point that the reader is already fully persuaded that, at least until 1833, Argentina held an irrefutable right of sovereignty over the Malvinas Islands and that the action of the HMS *Clio* was an act of force against their legitimate owner.

It would be unforgivable to omit reference to a series of important documents from the Ministry of Foreign Relations of the United Kingdom itself, which in terms of "one party's confessions" shed the most illuminating light imaginable.

The memoranda of 1910, 1928, and 1946. The documents in question are three Foreign Office memoranda whose existence and reason for being were mentioned briefly in the preliminary reflections to this essay. Hostilities awaken dormant concerns, sharpen the spirit of research, and bring to the surface of history events apparently buried forever. This is what happened with the conflict in the South Atlantic, and for this reason it is not surprising that copies of these important papers have been consulted by British researchers and that they are also safely stored in the archives of more than one Argentine expert.

For various reasons I do not share direct quotes from these documents, but limit myself to the references of British writers. In this connection, perhaps the contribution of greatest relevance from the work of Peter Beck might be his comments on the internal memoranda of the Foreign Office beginning with De Bernhardt's, written in 1910, revised in 1928, and concluding with something of a codification in 1946. It is clear that these are confidential internal documents of the Foreign Office and that as Beck indicates, the doubts that they contain "were confined to a small group of people," even in the British Foreign Office (S. 21, p. 51). He states at the same time that they "became an accepted British point of reference" (Ibid., p. 50). Let me briefly tell the story of their genesis and content.

At the turn of the century the Foreign Office, in view of Argentina's unflagging claims, instructed its assistant librarian De Bernhardt to prepare a study on the development of the dispute. Beck says that until then Great Britain, "treating sovereignty as non-negotiable and conscious of its power advantage, devoted little thought to either the topic or the alternative version advanced by its rival" (Ibid., p. 50).

In spite of the fact that De Bernhardt concentrated on the "facts" and not on the parties' merits, Beck believes: "To the reader, his history indicated various weaknesses in the traditional British case." Then he systematically enumerates those weak points:

- There appeared no certainty about the initial discovery.
- There was no prior British settlement.
- There had been only seven or eight years of British occupation before 1833.
- There were grounds for believing that any rights preserved by the 1774 plaque had lapsed with the passage of time; there existed evidence that prior to 1833 Argentina was in effective occupation of the islands.
- There was the implication that in 1833 Britain had seized control of a legitimate Argentine possession.

And he concludes:

> In practice, the memorandum cast the seeds of doubt and shook official confidence in the strength of a case taken for granted, indeed accepted uncritically, for a long time, even if occasional doubts had been voiced (those of the Duke of Wellington in 1829 and of the British Minister in Buenos Aires in 1885). (S. 21, p. 50)

The confidence of official circles appeared shattered since the assessment of the British Foreign Office practically coincided with the Argentine position. Is it possible to imagine anything more conclusive?

In the early 1930s, perhaps stimulated by renewed Argentine vigor in its campaign to regain possession of the Malvinas, the British Foreign Office resolved to undertake a new study. It concluded that the arguments centering on the discovery and on the settlement of Port Egmont were weak compared to peaceful British occupation, which was marking its centennial.

The weak British claims based on discovery and effective occupation received their coup de grace when the matter of the Malvinas was again taken up after World War II. In September 1946, the Foreign Office drew up a memorandum that contains an updating and codification of the British title to the islands. This very important document—just like the one from 1910—is still confidential, and I owe to Peter Beck my awareness of its existence and the use that I can make of its relevant information.

In homage to his hard work as a researcher, I will quote the essential parts that, as Beck states, offer "a revealing insight into the British attitudes of contemporary relevance":

> *Discovery.* The evidence substantiating British priority of discovery is not only insufficient, but irrelevant.
>
> *Occupation.* The British case for priority occupation before . . . the French (1764) is untenable, since the British occupation was not made effective until 1766.
>
> *The secret understanding of 1770.* If there were in fact a secret pledge in 1770, that would demolish the British case prior to 1833.
>
> *The leaden plaque of 1774.* The British did not return to the Falkland Islands for 60 years during which their claim may be deemed to have lapsed. (S. 21, p. 54)

I will return to the memorandum of 1946 in the next subchapter to prove that, in its last two sections, the Foreign Office constructs a new line of argument, setting aside the two elements—discovery and effective occupation—upon which Lord Palmerston based the piracy of 1833. This is the deed that, further in the same document, the British Foreign Office describes as "an act of unjustifiable aggression" (Ibid.).

This subchapter is dedicated to the circumstances of discovery and effective occupation, and I believe that British acknowledgment in this respect has been categorical, as illustrated by the opinions cited below.

The impact on British officials and experts' opinions. The repercussions of the memorandum of 1910 on Foreign Office officials themselves were enormous and brought about changes in position and a certain malaise because it made a mockery of their good faith. One official, Gerald Spicer, confessed at the end of 1910 that his confidence had evaporated and that the attitude of the Argentine government was not entirely unjustified. In 1911, another official, Ronald Campbell, accepted that the best claim without a doubt belonged to the United Provinces of the River Plate.

Similarly, the opinion of Sir Malcolm Robertson, the British ambassador in Buenos Aires, underwent a serious transformation when he learned—more than 15 years later—the content of the memorandum, and he wrote to the governor of the islands stating that the Argentine attitude was "neither ridiculous nor childish." He mentions the strength of the Argentine case and the weakness of the British. (S. 21, pp. 51–52)

Some years later, probably because of a consultation as to the wisdom of submitting the case to international arbitration, two other pronouncements were issued, also quoted by Beck, and because of their similar tenor I refer to them here.

Legal adviser Vyvian of the Foreign Office recognized in 1935 the uncertainty of a successful outcome if the case went to arbitration. The following year John Troutbeck, head of the Latin America Office, deemed the seizure of the islands in 1833 so arbitrary that it could not be explained except as the act of "international bandits."

These opinions of members of the Foreign Office logically had an impact on readers. Having sifted through the files of the Foreign Ministry and, among others, those of the United States Department of State as well, Beck concludes that after 1910 the British government perceived the weakness of its title over the Malvinas, although "of course, such doubts were never expressed publicly" (S. 24, p. 115). He concludes that Argentina has the "superior historical claim through inheritance and occupation" and that "privately, even British officials have admitted the latter's strength" (S. 21, p. 80).

HoCFAC

Malcolm Deas, summarizing in the memorandum presented to the Foreign Office his opinion on the historical background of the British seizure in 1833, says: "My conclusions are that the historical facts give Argentina a superior claim to Great Britain in that year" (S. 2, p. 127).

What more is there to write here when everything has been said so decisively? Perhaps no defense remains to the British other than the one Professor James Fawcett attempted so inappropriately for a jurist of his standing:

> In a situation like this, as in much international relations, law is really a question of tactics. . . . The law is more a matter of diplomacy. It is a question of advancing arguments which are politically reasonable and convincing. (S. 2, p. 139)

Of course, misuse of law as a tactic in favor of one's own interests entails the risk of burying one's head in the sand like an ostrich and realizing the seriousness of the case only when the cannons sound, staining with blood a dispute that never should have left the negotiating table. Clearly then, to negotiate the substance of the problem—that is, sovereignty over the islands—it is indispensable to have the political will, which according to Lord Franks's report was conspicuous by its absence in the United Kingdom during the years before the conflict in the South Atlantic.

ACQUISITIVE PRESCRIPTION

*The United Kingdom adopts prescription
as the basis for its title to the Malvinas.*

Given these increasing doubts concerning any claim it may have had to the islands prior to 1833, the British government was forced to shift its position. Accordingly, after the 1930s, and particularly after the celebration of the centennial of its occupation of the islands, it began to articulate its position in terms of a title founded on the passage of time since 1833, that is, by way of acquisitive prescription.

It is appropriate here to recall the new study undertaken at that time and to recall that interdepartmental discussions arrived at the conclusion "that previous arguments centered upon prior discovery and settlement, appeared relatively weak and inappropriate as compared to those emphasizing the length and peaceful nature of British occupation" (S. 21, p. 52).

Also at that time, the beginning of January 1933, the governor of the islands, probably counting on a clear pronouncement regarding the British titles in the midst of so much confusion, requested to be "enlightened as to the general policy" in the Malvinas. The Colonial Office, in a dispatch dated November 13 of that year, answered that it was unnecessary to discuss British title in more detail: "His Majesty's government were advised that that title, while unquestionably strong, is based mainly upon the right of prescription." The position was structured on this basis, and by 1934 a diplomat summed it up, saying, "Our best title is of prescription." (S. 20, pp. 8–9; Mason, 8/29/34, FO371/17474/A6881)

Five decades later, in July 1982, following the armed conflict of that year, British Foreign Minister Francis Pym confirmed the validity of this argument: "Our title can be soundly based on our possession of the islands from 1833. . . . Prescription as a mode of acquiring territory is generally recognized in international law" (S. 21, p. 46).

While there are experts in international law, among them Britishers, who state that prescription—originating in private law—lacks general validity in international law (R. Jennings, *The Acquisition of Territory in International Law,* Manchester, 1963, p. 20; I. Brownlie, *Principles of Public International Law,* 1979, p. 163), it is not my purpose here to flatly reject this principle in the Malvinas case. But without a doubt what must be analyzed is whether British possession of the islands after 1833 fills the requirements stipulated in international law as to the acquisition of legitimate title by acquisitive prescription.

It is not necessary to emphasize the importance of this point, because acquisitive prescription, and the principle of self-determination later added to it, are still today the principal, if not the only legal, grounds upon which the United Kingdom claims rights over the Malvinas Islands.

The elements of prescription.

In October 1946, the legal adviser to the Foreign Office, William Beckett, offered a definition that, according to my method of relying on British sources, I should cite here:

> Occupation is a method of acquiring title to territory which is "terra nullius" [no-man's land], and prescription is a means of acquiring territory which originally belonged to somebody else and whose title is destroyed by the fact that the acquirer has successfully maintained possession. (S. 21, p. 46)

Clearly, this definition has been transparently adapted to further the British cause in the Malvinas.

Validating the current application of prescription, the memorandum of the Foreign Office dated December 17, 1982, maintains that prescription is the acquisition of territory that is not terra nullius, by virtue of a long period of possession. It adds that writers distinguish between acquisitive and extinguishing prescription:

> Title by "acquisitive prescription" arises out of long-continued possession where no original source of title can be shown to exist or where possession in the first instance is in the face of an adverse title and the legitimate proprietor has taken no measures to assert his right or has been unable to do so. (S. 2, p. 149)

It is evident that the Foreign Office is trying to hide the flaws in the legal merits of its case prior to 1833 in its wish to put forward a title accepted by and, presumably, acceptable to the international community.

I suggest that the subject is complex and demands careful analysis. In order not to depart from my method, I cite a British source who identifies and analyzes the elements that come into play in acquisitive prescription in the specific context of the dispute over the Malvinas. Peter Beck says the elements are the following:

- the period of time necessary for the acquisitive prescription (between 12 and 100 years);
- whether an initially illegal occupation can ever be validated; or
- whether continuing protest by the dispossessed party prevents the assumption of legal title. (S. 21, p. 46)

Applied to the Malvinas question, it is obvious that the first require-ment, the passage of time, is undisputed. But compliance with the two re-maining elements remains to be seen: whether an illegal act can be the source of any right and whether possession was peaceful, meaning uncon-tested, in particular by the party questioning the legitimacy of the title.

British occupation as an illegal act of aggression that has not been validated by the passage of time. It is relevant here to note what happened in the is-lands in January 1833 when Captain Onslow in command of the HMS *Clio* forced Captain Pinedo to abandon the Malvinas, raised the English colors, and took possession of the islands in the name of the British Crown. The nature of this act is one of the elements crucial to the determination of title to the Malvinas.

In the previous subchapter we saw how the volume of the Royal In-stitute of International Affairs (RIIA) on South America, a "semiofficial" source, said in its original version that the islands had been "annexed by force." In light of the facts, that is the only possible interpretation of the occupation of 1833.

Similarly, Jeffrey Myhre does not hesitate to confirm the illegality of the 1833 act, saying: "Since it is almost indisputable that Argentina had title to the islands when the British took them in 1833, that invasion can-not be anything but an illegal act of aggression" (S. 18, p. 33).

Few can deny that the statements of Gerald Fitzmaurice, veteran legal adviser to the Foreign Office, constitute a special "confession by the other party." Based on his discovery and reading of an internal memorandum, Peter Beck, commenting on the weaknesses of the British title, maintains that there are "not only doubts about the priority of British discovery and settlement, but also about the possibility that in 1833 Britain had expelled a legitimate Argentine occupation of the islands" (Fitzmaurice's minutes dated February 6, 1936; FO 371/19763 as cited by Beck, S. 20, p. 11).

On this question, British admissions can be seen as virtually categori-cal, since the preceding opinion can be added to the very confidential For-eign Office memorandum of 1946, which termed the usurpation of 1833 "an unjustifiable act of aggression."

I could close this subsection now were it not that the document in question, after accepting the illicit nature of the possessory act, adds that it "has now acquired the backing of the right of prescription" (S. 21, p. 46).

The reasoning is clear: The claim to legitimate title is founded on an illegal act of aggression but with the passage of time has become legiti-mate. But can this be? Is such a claim valid, even by British standards?

The reputable jurist Ian Brownlie, in a work on the use of force by states maintains: "It is arguable that as a matter of principle the initial illegality can never be the source of legal right" (*International Law and the Use of Force by States,* Oxford University Press, Oxford, 1963, p. 422).

Beck and Deas share Professor Brownlie's opinion. Deas, in the memorandum he submitted to the Kershaw Committee, says of the arguments validating prescription:

> Assuming that title can result from adverse possession, the general recognition that the use of force as an instrument of national policy is illegal must cause such derivation to title to occur only in rare cases as a result of very long possession of general acquiescence by the international community. If prescription is permissible in such circumstances, explicit statement as to non-recognition could play the role of protest in preventing or delaying the prescriptive process. (S. 2, p. 129)

In any event, none of these circumstances is present in the Malvinas matter, which certainly does not qualify as one of those "rare cases" to which Deas refers. This is why he concludes, based on Brownlie, that "it is probably the law that prescription cannot create rights out of situations brought about by illegal acts" (*Principles of Public International Law,* 1979, p. 161; S. 2, p. 129).

Even Professor Fawcett, asked by the Kershaw Committee whether the doctrine of prescription depends "on the way in which the territory was acquired in the first place," answered, "I think it would, yes." He added that for this reason he attributes importance to the argument that the 1833 occupation "was not unlawful." The following dialogue ensued:

> *Sir Hooley:* But if it was held to be unlawful by somebody or bodies, then the prescription rule would not apply?
> *Mr. Fawcett:* I think it would be so, the prescription rule, yes. (S. 2, p. 141)

In summary, the British occupation in the Malvinas in 1833 was an illegal act of aggression. As such, it suffers from an incurable flaw that allows, in and of itself, the rejection of prescription as a source of the legitimacy of British titles. However, let us examine the remaining element required for the application of the prescription principle.

British possession was not peaceful, uninterrupted, and uncontested. Among the elements of a title based on acquisitive prescription is that possession must have been peaceful, that is, not weakened by express lack of acquiescence on the part of the previous occupant. In this context, international law experts confirm that the latter's protests are sufficient to interrupt prescription (Brownie lecture, op. cit., p. 160; I.F.L. Oppenheim, *International Law,* vol. 1, 8th ed., p. 576; Paul Fauchille, *Traité de Droit International,* vol. 1, p. 760).

As indicated by Mr. Canavan, member of the Kershaw Committee, basing his statement on international law: "Full rights of prescription are only achieved with the acquiescence of the other claimant" (S. 2, p. 164).

In the specific context of the Malvinas, Jeffrey Myhre notes that in order to acquire title through possession, a "state can show it has . . . exercised its authority in a continuous, uninterrupted and peaceful manner . . . provided that all other interested and affected States . . . have acquiesced in the exercise of such authority" (S. 18, p. 33). And he correctly maintains that Great Britain must prove this.

The normal procedure for interrupting prescription is through diplomatic protests by the state from which the territory was taken. It is not surprising that the Kershaw Committee asked the Foreign Office whether such protests had been lodged. In a December 17, 1983, memorandum, the Foreign Ministry answered:

> The Argentine government formally protested about the British occupation of the Falkland Islands in 1833, 1834, 1841, 1842, 1849, 1884, and 1888. During this century Argentina has, in official correspondence with HMG and in many fora, repeatedly placed on record her claim to the Falklands. (S. 2, pp. 148–149, question 11)

Systematic lack of any British response doubtless produced feelings of impotence and frustration and during certain periods may have discouraged the pressing of Argentina's claims. There were in particular two periods of silence (1849–1884 and 1888–1908). Deas, however, is of the opinion that despite these gaps, "Argentine diplomatic protest may be regarded as continuous since 1833" (S. 2, p. 139, question 7). Myhre also attaches little value to these two periods because of "the fact that Argentina stressed in 1849 that the lack of protest in future should not be taken to mean that it has abandoned its claim" (S. 18, p. 34). Myhre is correct because the reservation of rights as formulated by Argentina is fully recognized under international law.

Beck also justifies Argentina's conduct, saying: "However, domestic preoccupations, in association with its clear naval and economic inferiority, forced Argentina to rely on diplomacy to encourage Britain either to negotiate or, as suggested in 1884, to accept arbitration" (S. 21, pp. 89–90). Precisely this willingness to submit the case to a legal determination is sufficient to outweigh any silence.

British archives reveal that, given the aggressiveness of the Colonial Office and other sectors of the government, the Foreign Office was normally the moderating element, which took into account the totality of bilateral relations with Argentina and gave preference, when it deemed necessary, to the latter in incidents related to the policy in the Malvinas.

It is clear to the researcher, as Beck notes, that the arguments of Argentine sectors also interested in preserving economic ties were at times influential and were "the heart of the matter." More than once, as has happened even today, they pressured government circles to calm the media and public opinion in general, in order to prevent the Malvinas matter from being agitated in such a way as to affect their commercial interests.

After this brief digression—which is necessary to the understanding of certain periods in the history of the Malvinas—and to conclude, let us return to Malcolm Deas's comments. Referring to the British argument of so-called "acquisitive prescription," he disqualifies it in these terms: "We have our prescription argument . . . which is somewhat tricky because it will be an adverse prescription, that is, against a continual stream of Argentine protests . . . and there are different views about the validity of the argument." And he judges the behavior of his country as follows:

> This was part of our imperial expansion and we took a bit of their territory because it was of great naval potential at that time . . . and the Argentines then protested . . . and have protested pretty well ever since one way or another that they want it back and, therefore, what they say is that this is an imperial relic. (S. 2, p. 136)

In any case, in order to legitimize the "imperial relic" it would be necessary to resort to Fawcett's "tactics," putting effective occupation and uninterrupted British administration above all else, or to rely on the argument of Sir Ian Sinclair, legal adviser to the Foreign Office, who is of the opinion that a party's lack of acquiescence does not obviate the process of prescription. Unfortunately for the United Kingdom's case, other British experts all express the opposite opinion, and, they are joined by treatise writers around the world.

Therefore, with regard to the Malvinas question, of the three elements Beck identifies as indispensable requirements for acquiring title to sovereignty through the institution of prescription, two are lacking. Certainly the United Kingdom would not be able to invoke the doctrine with any success in any international court, and I am convinced that Fawcett as well as Sinclair know this very well. It was not in vain that the former stated to the Kershaw Committee: "To stand simply on prescription may not carry you very far" (S. 2, p. 141).

I fully support this last conclusion of the legal adviser to the British Foreign Office and believe that I have demonstrated why.

SELF-DETERMINATION

British emphasis on self-determination
as a basis for its refusal
to transfer sovereignty.

Anyone familiar with the Argentine-British discussions on the Malvinas question doubtless knows of the increased and negative role the principle of self-determination has assumed, as advanced by the United Kingdom in an effort to bolster its exceedingly weak juridical position. Indeed, that the United Kingdom now falls back on self-determination is an indication of just how empty its other arguments are.

In this subchapter I will demonstrate that the "principle of self-determination" has no legal, academic, or even political application in the context of the dispute over the sovereignty of the Malvinas Islands. This, however, has not kept it from becoming the major obstacle to a negotiated solution. Indeed, it still clouds the possibilities of any long-term understanding regarding the institutional future of the three southern archipelagoes in controversy.

Once again Peter Beck provides the first British observations, which confirm my initial thoughts:

> The British government has attempted recently to move the discussion on to other factors, most notably towards an emphasis upon the "paramountcy" of the Islanders' freely-expressed wishes to remain British, which "take priority over any other interests involved," including Argentina's abstract historical rights. (HCFAC, 1982–83, 2/21/83, p. 391, Onslow; S. 21, pp. 48–49)

In recent years the concept of self-determination—given in Articles 1 and 73 of the United Nations Charter—has been emphasized among the factors that at one time or another influenced the thoughts of the British government. Beck defends this change—or "shift"—and points out that "the right to self-determination which is now an important part of our case has emerged only relatively recently as a principle of international law" (S. 21, p. 55).

Naturally, as it is alleged that its weight has become so great that it acquires priority over any other element of judgment—including Argentina's historical rights, which now are branded "abstract"—I feel obligated to duly enlighten the reader. I will do this first with regard to the principle in and of itself—its nature and characteristics—and second with regard to the alleged application to the Malvinas question. As usual, I will rely on the opinion of British writers.

Conceptualization of the principle: History.
Political axiom or legal concept.

In an article published in 1983 on the application of the principle to the Malvinas, Denzil Dunnett, a diplomat who retired after 30 years of service in the Foreign Office, traces its history. He says that the concept has Anglo-Saxon origins and is far from universal in its application. He notes that it was President Woodrow Wilson who first enunciated the idea in his famous speech of July 4, 1918: "Every territorial settlement involved in this War must be made in the interest and for the benefit of the population concerned. Self-determination . . . is an imperative principle of action" (S. 10, p. 416).

Without disparaging the great attraction this principle has held in spirit, I submit that as a political instrumentality it is complex and must be handled with care. Even at the time of its launching, Robert Lansing, secretary of state under Wilson, stated: "The phrase is simply loaded with dynamite. . . . What a calamity that the phrase was ever uttered" (Ibid., p. 417).

I do not share this assessment in any way, given that this "calamity" has permitted an end to the colonial status of dozens of peoples who, under its generous invocation, were able to obtain their independence.

It is certainly not surprising that the colonial powers themselves, including the United Kingdom, have been the first to have problems with the concept. How could self-determination be a legal obligation—they said— "when no definition has been established of such terms as 'people,' 'nation,' and 'the right to self-determination'?" (Ibid., p. 423)

Given the problems with self-determination—according to British sources—it is paradoxical that so many sacred flames have been ignited now in the United Kingdom for its application in the Malvinas, although it has not been this way in every case. Some of this British questioning is relevant and works against the British in the sovereignty dispute over the southern archipelagoes.

What is happening is that the United Kingdom, surely conscious of the weakness of its position in the context of international law, has departed— by means of pronouncements from its political and academic sectors— from legal arguments and is leaning toward the principle that I am analyzing, which is essentially identified as a political axiom.

On this question of the nature of the principle, let us focus attention on the words of Myhre and Beck. The former, commenting on the new factors—self-determination and decolonization—which emerged after World War II and which can have an influence on the title, acknowledges that "doubts exist as to whether these are principles in international law or something more politically motivated" (S. 18, p. 35). Beck also notes that "in addition, self-determination, lacking in case of law, is often interpreted as a political axiom . . . not a legal concept. . . . It has no strength in international law but a great strength in international relations" (S. 21, p. 49).

The reader should note these observations well because, when in the resolution of an international controversy law is put aside in favor of an attempt at a political solution, it happens within the parameters of power, which have historically been negative for the weaker party.

The principle of self-determination and the Malvinas question.

Because the principle I am analyzing is the most decisive obstacle to the solution of the dispute over sovereignty in the southern archipelagoes, the question of its relevance takes on special significance. All the more so taking into account the extremes to which the British, particularly the Conservative administration, go in defending its validity in this case.

On the other hand, the Argentines—who have consistently supported, even promoted, its application in every genuine process of decolonization in which it was invoked—maintain that:

   i. The principle of self-determination is not applicable to the Malvinas case because it would be a violation of the principle of territorial integrity.

   ii. The correct application of the principle assumes taking into consideration the interests of the population; thus the interpretation propounded by certain British sectors that gives priority to the wishes of the population in any agreement as to the future of the islands, is incorrect.

   iii. It is arguable whether the population of the islands constitutes "a people" within the meaning of the United Nations Charter and the Declaration of 1960.

I will successively develop these three Argentine arguments through admissions from British sources.

Self-determination vis-à-vis territorial integrity. In December 1960, the United Nations General Assembly—after arduous negotiations—finally adopted Resolution 1514 (XV) containing the "Declaration on the Concession of Independence to Colonial Countries and Peoples," which gives an exact dimension to the principle of self-determination consecrated by Article 73 of the Charter. In doing this, it recognized that this concept, incorrectly handled, could cause serious political problems, such as the territorial dismemberment of states to the detriment of their national unity. For this reason the text of this important resolution incorporates a dispositive paragraph: "Sixth. Every intent, partial or total, to disrupt the unity or the territorial integrity of a country is incompatible with the purposes and principles of the Charter of the United Nations."

This provision is of great significance in our case, given that Argentina has consistently argued against the application of the principle of self-determination to the Malvinas question, precisely because it would violate the principle of territorial integrity, which the United Nations had determined a specific exception to it.

As Dunnett notes, the doctrine was first set forth with greatest precision in Resolution 2353 (XXII), adopted in 1967, which states: "Any colonial situation which, partially or completely, destroys the national unity or territorial integrity of a country is incompatible with the purposes and principles of the Charter" (S. 10, p. 425).

Dunnett, a product of the British Foreign Office, cites cases in which the principle of territorial integrity was imposed over the principle of self-determination. Among them he mentions Hong Kong—a case that is curiously relevant to the Malvinas question—in which the territorial integrity of China took absolute priority over self-determination. And he candidly concludes: "There is no point in not recognizing that the U.N. has on occasion allowed precedence over self-determination to other considerations, in particular territorial integrity." And as to self-determination, he adds: "The problem is to find a proper place for this previous element, without either making it into an absolute imperative or relegating it to insignificance." (Ibid., pp. 425–426)

I agree with Dunnett's interpretation, but not with his partial application of principles. Argentina understands that the "proper place" he speaks of would mean ensuring the interests of the population of the islands. But Argentina does not believe that the principle of self-determination applies to the southern archipelagoes, which are the subject of this essay, territories that were usurped in violation of territorial integrity.

The "wishes" versus the "interests" of the Islanders. Although the position previously summarized would make any other argument unnecessary, I do not want to evade a debate on British terrain, meaning an examination of the principles the United Kingdom considers applicable.

These assume, on one hand, reference to the pertinent articles in the United Nations Charter and, on the other, the specific framework adopted in the case of the Malvinas. When I have commented on both, the reader will harbor no doubts. Both are conclusive and do not lend themselves to the interpretation that the wishes of the population have the last word as to the final destiny of the southern archipelagoes.

We will begin with the specific framework of the Malvinas. In 1964, Argentina for the first time took to the United Nations—specifically to the Committee on Decolonization—the Malvinas question, in the context of Resolution 1514 (XV). Then, also for the first time, a controversy arose with the United Kingdom as to whether—within the framework of negotiations over the sovereignty dispute as proposed in the resolution—the *desires* of the Islanders should be taken into account, as the British wanted, or only their *interests.*

The Argentine position gained acceptance in this forum, known as the Committee of 24, and also the following year in Resolution 2065 (XX), adopted by the General Assembly on December 16, 1965, which invited the parties to negotiate without delay, and which stipulated that the "interests" of the Islanders be taken into account. Beck correctly comments that "its emphasis upon the 'interests' rather than the 'wishes' of the Islanders qualified the prospects for the implementation of the self-determination principle." In a philosophical vein, he goes on to note that

> in effect, a nineteenth century theoretical claim was accepted as a twentieth century international issue in spite of the efforts of a British government, prepared to discuss the peaceful development of Anglo-Argentine relations in general but critical of the attempt to employ the U.N. framework for a non-negotiable dispute. And thus it abstained rather than support the Resolution. (S. 21, p. 97)

In any event, it is the concept of the interests, and not the wishes, of the population of the Malvinas that the United Nations has addressed in the specific treatment set forth in resolutions relevant to this case.

Regarding the general framework, it is a fact that the United Nations Charter in Article 73 (e) speaks of the interests of the people involved in self-determination. In that context the position that the Kershaw Committee assumed in the draft report on policy in the Malvinas published on May 11, 1983, is, in my judgment, very significant. In point 2.27 it states that "although Article 73 of the U.N. Charter is written in terms of the 'paramountcy' of the Islanders' interests, rather than their wishes, an additional obligation is placed on Britain to take due account of the political aspirations" of the population. And it concludes: "Your Committee believes that HM government's determination that no change in the administration and government of the Falkland Islands should be agreed to without the fullest consideration of the views of the Islanders." (S. 4, p. xxvii)

This statement represents something akin to a reinforced version of respect for the interests of the population, but cannot be interpreted as authorizing an island veto. The statement subsequently clarifies the point by stating that the terminology employed by the British ministers has not always been consistent, and the suggestion that the Islanders' wishes are and will remain "paramount" could be regarded within the United Kingdom itself as unacceptable in view of the ultimate and sovereign responsibility of Parliament to approve any settlement regarding the Islands' future. (Ibid.)

Dunnett, commenting specifically on Mrs. Thatcher's position that any solution must safeguard the principle that the wishes of the Islanders must be supreme, says that not all of the members of the Lower House, even those sympathetic to the government, are in agreement. He notes that the great conservative leader Edward Heath—although he basically supported the policy toward the islands—took another line on the subject of self-determination. Asked by a colleague in the course of a parliamentary debate whether what he had said was that the principle of self-determination was not applicable to the Falkland Islands, he answered, "Yes, that is correct, and I have said that before" (S. 10, p. 415).

In summary, given what is established by the applicable legal framework, meaning the United Nations Charter and the resolutions approved on the Malvinas; what is maintained in the draft report of the Kershaw Commission of the House of Commons; the views of British academicians whose opinions we have transcribed; the opinions of respected political leaders—E. Heath preceded M. Thatcher as head of the Tory Party—I think the reader must be as convinced as I am of an indisputable point: In the long-term solution to the future of the southern archipelagoes, what must be contemplated is the interests of the Islanders.

To leave totally in their hands—that is, according to their "wishes"—the result of Anglo-Argentine negotiations would be an act of absolute political irresponsibility in view of the great and irreparable damage to life and property that this approach has cost the two countries involved.

The concept of "a people" as related to the self-determination of the population of the islands. According to various United Nations texts, including the Declaration of 1960, all peoples have the right to self-determination. That is, the right in question is to be exercised by a "people."

Ivor Jennings, a respected British authority on constitutional law, states that at first this principle appeared reasonable, but that "the people cannot decide until somebody decides who are the 'people'" (S. 10, p. 417).

What do the experts think of this? According to Dunnett, in his work cited above, "Very small countries have certainly been given independence but it is doubtful if the inhabitants of the Falkland Islands would be considered to be 'a people' in this sense" (Ibid., pp. 417–418). Why? There are several reasons, some of which in principle bear on—according to British sources—the characteristics of the human beings residing in the Malvinas.

A first consideration would be their number, which is small and moreover declining, among other characteristics and tendencies. In this connection Beck says, "The population rose gradually from 287 in 1851 to 2,392 in 1931, before declining to 1,921 in 1972 and 1,813 in 1980; in addition, the population assumed increasingly an unbalanced age and sex distribution, a situation aggravated by emigration and restrictions on immigration" (S. 21, p. 45). Moreover, nearly a quarter are temporary residents, connected to the islands for a few years only by virtue of contracts.

All this might have been expected to change after 1982, particularly with the military presence established in the islands. However, from the point of view of this analysis, there are no significant variations; the new residents are mostly contract employees, and few changes have been observed in the number and composition of the "Kelpers," the population truly native to the islands.

Another circumstance exists that seriously invalidates application of the principle of self-determination in the Malvinas. If the population's homogeneity has been preserved, it has been at the price of prohibiting Argentines from immigrating to the islands, acquiring land, or making investments. Sir Richard Hunt, when questioned by the Kershaw Committee on these points, admitted that "for practical purposes local people had a veto on either land acquisition or immigration" (S. 3, pp. 196–197).

There is no doubt that one of the most irritating and arbitrary aspects of the position of the United Kingdom is the limitation on free immigration of Argentine people and capital to the islands. This is a basic right that the British enjoy in Argentina, and the fact that Argentines cannot migrate or acquire property and that there is no free movement of people and capital has frozen the situation in the Malvinas. The existing community is not the result of the exercise of these essential rights but of their limitation. And this freeze over a period of 150 years reduces the legal significance of the "wishes" of a population that would be fundamentally different if the norms of civilized communities were applicable to the islands.

This has been the understanding of the international community, which recently rejected the application of self-determination in the Malvinas question. The setting of this Argentine victory was the United Nations General Assembly, which had the opportunity to make a pronouncement at the request of British diplomats who had erred in their calculations. In 1985, in fact, the United Kingdom proposed two amendments to the text of one of the numerous draft resolutions submitted to the world forum. This one called for the resolution of the sovereignty dispute through negotiations. The British amendments—a paragraph in the preamble to the resolution and an addition to the first substantive paragraph—sought to incorporate language referring to "the right of peoples to free determination established in the Charter," as stated word for word in the second amendment.

Both amendments were firmly rejected, which constitutes an explicit message from the international community on the inapplicability of the principle to the controversy over the sovereignty of the southern archipelagoes (Appendix 1).

If we combine this fact with the "confessions" described above, it is clear that (1) the British position places the wishes of the Islanders at the vertex of the factors that must converge in any solution to this legendary controversy, and (2) that this is unacceptable to the international community.

Great Britain subordinates self-determination to strategic interests: The case of Diego García Island.

One of the members of the Kershaw Committee, Mr. Foulkes, requested the undersecretary to report whether the principle of self-determination had been applied to other overseas dependencies. He specifically asked, "What was the thinking of the Foreign Office in the case of Diego García?" Mr. Hooley presided at the hearing and the following dialogue ensued:

> *Mr. Hooley:* I must rule that out of order, we are dealing with the Falklands.
>
> *Mr. Foulkes:* It's directly related.
>
> *Mr. Hooley:* With respect, it is not. We are not discussing Diego García at the moment.
>
> *Mr. Foulkes:* I would record my dissent and concern that we are not able to ask questions which are related. We are talking about the Falkland Islands in relation to various dependencies which the United Kingdom has responsibility for. If we are looking at the future of the Falkland Islands, we cannot look at it in isolation; we have to look at Hong Kong and Gibraltar.
>
> *Mr. Hooley:* Can we move to the next question? (S. 4, p. 35)

The reader will note the abrupt tone of the preceding dialogue. The case of Diego García Island is one that any nation that respects human rights would rather forget, and all the more so in the context of the Malvinas question. Why particularly in this case? Well, because in Diego García the United Kingdom placed its strategic interests ahead of the wishes of the population of the island, who were never consulted, nor was the principle of self-determination invoked in their case.

In discussions with the United Kingdom in multilateral fora, Argentina has brought up this case more than once to demonstrate that adhesion to the principle of self-determination is not a sacred norm of international conduct on the part of the United Kingdom, as it sometimes claims when discussing the Malvinas case.

I am going to illustrate briefly the "deplorable" events—as Lord Brockway terms them—that placed Diego García on the agenda of the Minority Rights Group of the House of Lords in a distressing session held November 11, 1982, an important year in the history of the southern archipelagoes. In keeping with my method, I will limit myself to information or commentaries excerpted from British sources, in this case from the Official Reports of the Upper House (S. 26, vol. 426, no. 5, pp. 398–402).

Let us look at the background of the case. In 1965, the British government offered Mauritius its independence but on the condition that it surrender the Chagos archipelago, of which Diego García is the largest island, measuring 15 by 4 miles. Three million pounds in compensation was offered to the government of Mauritius. But the latter did not accept the treaty offered on those terms and took the case to the United Nations, which, in Resolution 2066 (XX) of the General Assembly, recommended taking "no action which could dismember the territory of Mauritius and violate its territorial integrity."

The first similarity with Malvinas was the violation of the principle of territorial identity. But the similarities do not end there, for the number of inhabitants was also comparable: 1,800 inhabitants with a similar monoculture and colonial structure. One difference in Mauritius was the presence of people of color: 60 percent were of African origin (from the continent or Madagascar) and 40 percent were Indian.

In the end, certainly under pressure, Mauritius accepted the offer. Later, Lord Brockway, introducing the subject in the House, termed this extraordinary: "The British government without any consultation of the people incorporated Diego García into a new colony, the British Indian Ocean Territory. It is known as BIOT" And he continued: "The object of this strange maneuver became clear the following year. . . . The U.S. wanted BIOT and particularly Diego García because it had been selected by the Pentagon as an ideal place to monitor the Soviet Navy.

The Pentagon made clear that it wanted no one but U.S. personnel in the islands, and it asked the United Kingdom to remove the local residents. Brockway says: "Africans and Indians yes, but British citizens. They were just tossed out at the dictates of Whitehall."

Procedures were expeditious. Those "Llois"—as the "Kelpers" of Diego García were called—who left the islands on vacation found no ship upon which to return. By 1967, the only employer on the island had been bought out; in 1973, the cocoa plantation had to close down. The manager admitted that it was not very agreeable for him to obey the orders from BIOT: "I am talking about five generations of Llois who were buried there." According to the report of the Minority Rights Group, the next step was to cut off the food supply. The local population was left only with fish, coconuts, and vegetables "in order to starve them out." The first U.S.

personnel arrived in the islands in 1971 and the Llois were given two weeks in which to leave. BIOT shipped them out in their own boats.

In the final analysis, once again during the last third of the twentieth century, the United Kingdom did not appear to ardently defend the principle of self-determination of the Llois the way it does today for the Kelpers. And there is another similarity with the Malvinas case. Just as in 1833, when plunder by force was termed persuasion by the Foreign Office, on this occasion as well—according to Lord Brockway—the interpretation was that the natives went willingly and no coercion was used. It is difficult for me, as it is for my British informant, to believe that was the case.

I believe that this account taken from the Sessions Diary of the House of Lords sufficiently illustrates that the principle of self-determination is not as sacred to the British ruling class as it claims. Particularly, it is inescapable that this principle loses currency in the United Kingdom when it is weighed against strategic values. Lord Brockway concludes without subterfuge: "First, there is evidence that the confrontation between the West and the Soviet Union ostensibly in defense of democracy and freedom rides roughshod over these values in order to obtain military advantage, as in Diego García." As we shall see in the last chapter of this essay, this conclusion also takes on great importance in the question of the Malvinas where the strategic variable is not unknown.

Lord Brockway's second conclusion refers concretely to the Malvinas case, which he says cannot be more relevant in view of the great expense and loss of life accepted in the name of the self-determination of an approximately equal number of persons.

His third conclusion also relates specifically to the Malvinas question. On behalf of governments in the area expressing this desire, he calls for the ocean to become a zone of peace. And he asks, "If the British government sincerely desires disarmament in the world, cannot it support this demilitarization?" As is well known, the United Nations has also recommended the establishment of a zone of peace in the South Atlantic.

Lord Brockway's last conclusion also belongs here, because the government is being asked to rectify a "crime" of which both parties—he said—were guilty. "We have all been guilty and we should all seek to right the wrong."

The rectification of wrongs, in international politics as in any other field, is possible. It requires courage, which makes it the privilege of peoples with a spirit of greatness. We are convinced that more than a few citizens of the United Kingdom are aware that the past and present policy in the Malvinas is an error. We hope that this spirit of greatness will pave the way to sealing the friendship of two nations which, perhaps in an excess of courage, were protagonists in an armed conflict that caught the world by surprise.

EVALUATION: THE LEGITIMACY
AND SUPERIORITY OF ARGENTINE TITLES

Throughout this chapter we have seen how the United Kingdom currently recognizes the extreme weakness of its historical and legal titles, particularly as regards the first establishment of effective occupation in the Malvinas Islands and also as regards its pretensions to a right of sovereignty founded on acquisitive prescription.

The conclusion arrived at by Peter Beck should serve as our colophon:

> Because historical and legal factors provide no compelling reason for an unyielding British stand on the sovereignty question, attention is focused upon the impact of policy reasons related to self-determination and the wishes of the Islanders. (S. 21)

This is confirmed by the most relevant and most current documentary proof we can offer: the report of the Kershaw Committee of 1984, which maintains that the United Kingdom answered Argentine claims not with the defense of its legal titles but "with an assertion of Britain's legal, political and moral obligation to the population of the Falkland Islands in her role as the recognized administering power for the territory (under Article 73 of the U.N. Charter) and the rights of the Falklanders to self-determination (under Article 1 of the Charter)."

This shift in the British position is enormously significant, because through it the United Kingdom seeks to set aside all debate as to who has the best title to the islands. It does not matter who has it; what counts is that the Islanders, since they cannot be independent, prefer to be British. In this way they appear to have found a way out of the dilemma that has preoccupied us throughout this first chapter.

The current British position has been reduced to this argument, which suffers from a great weakness as regards its applicability to the Malvinas question. The quid pro quo now is that leaving the rationality of law we enter into realpolitik, power politics. Peter Beck bluntly states in his memorandum to the Kershaw Committee: "Power and will are the decisive considerations, when it comes to the crunch. Similarly, power and will are likely to prove the major determinants of the durability of British rule over the Falklands" (S. 4, p. 116).

It might be illegal, it might be unfair, and in some cases it might even be immoral, but power politics is a permanent feature of international relations, and no politician can handle the foreign policy of his or her country without the variable in the decisionmaking mechanism that defines the course of action proposed for execution. It is this that also must be kept clearly in mind and to which we will return later.

2

The Second British Dilemma: Its Implicit Recognition of Argentina's Rights over the Southern Archipelagoes

BRITISH PROPOSALS AS TESTIMONY TO THE LEGITIMACY OF ARGENTINA'S RIGHTS

The report that the Foreign Affairs Committee of the House of Commons chaired by Lord Kershaw adopted in 1984 says in point 29:

> In March 1967, having failed to reach agreement on a freeze in discussions over sovereignty, the British government for the first time formally informed Argentina that they would be prepared to cede sovereignty over the islands under certain conditions. (S. 6, p. XVIII)

Peter Beck explains the importance of this fact:

> Since the late 1960s, a succession of British governments have been moving towards a transfer of sovereignty, even at the price of placing themselves at a distance from the islands and parliamentary opinion. Both Labour and Conservative governments have demonstrated and increased their preparedness . . . to treat sovereignty as negotiable. (S. 9, p. 45)

Could one think of a clearer confession on the British side as to the unassailability of Argentina's rights over the Malvinas Islands? This recognition—which we shall see also includes the southern archipelagoes of the South Georgias and the South Sandwich Islands—undeniably emerges from the various proposals that for 15 years—from 1967 to 1981—the

United Kingdom placed on the negotiating table with Argentina. Protected by the confidentiality of the negotiating process, these proposals were not disclosed to the peoples involved, Argentine or British. We owe it to Lord Franks that they became public in his well-known report.

I consider this a positive step—in the first place because, given the seriousness of the 1982 hostilities, the international community deserves to know the whole truth, or at least the two peoples directly involved should know. Perhaps if the British people had known the true story of the islands, they would have doubted the wisdom of undertaking acts of belligerence of such magnitude in a questionable cause.

In the second place, it is inescapable that the United Kingdom's proposals, discussed for years with Argentine negotiators, include an implicit acknowledgment of, and are conclusive testimony to, the legitimacy of the Argentine Republic's title to the southern archipelagoes. At least, as one of the members of the Kershaw Committee said ironically, British sovereignty over the islands is not as certain as British sovereignty over the city of London. If it were, it would be inconceivable for the United Kingdom to have formulated several initiatives for their transfer to Argentina. (S. 2, p. 169) If by chance the tables were turned, would Argentina be willing to negotiate the sovereignty of Isla de los Estados (Argentinian islands at the tip of Tierra del Fuego)?

Britain's prolonged willingness to negotiate the sovereignty of the islands, in my opinion, takes on a very special relevance, because it suggests that from a legal point of view, the legitimacy of Argentine claims were not changed by the armed conflict of 1982. Lord Kershaw himself suggested this when he questioned Baroness Young, the assistant secretary of state, and correctly pointed out that before the conflict the Foreign Office was prepared to discuss sovereignty, "but essentially all that has changed is the conflict, and its aftermath, not the principle that we were prepared to negotiate sovereignty" (S. 5, p. 136).

As I stated in my reflections in the prologue, I impute such importance to the political implications of the various British proposals that the mere fact of bringing them to light chronologically and systematically, as I do in this chapter, justifies the effort in writing the essay.

*Transfer of sovereignty subject to respect
for the interests of the population of the Malvinas.*

The first Anglo-Argentine discussions on sovereignty over the islands. Since the early 1960s—more specifically since Bonifacio del Carril assumed his post as foreign minister—Argentina has not wavered in its effort to recover its rights to the Malvinas Islands. This zeal continued under the leadership of President Illia's foreign minister, Miguel Angel Závala Ortiz. The Franks Report acknowledges that "in 1963 and 1964 there was a resurgence of Argentine interest in the Falklands and a campaign was mounted in Argentina in support of its claim to the islands" (S. 1, p. 4).

Argentina took its claim to the United Nations for the first time in 1964. There it obtained massive support through the General Assembly's adoption of Resolution 2065 (XX) on December 16, 1965, the first resolution specifically on the Malvinas question adopted by the highest forum of the organization. Essentially, this called on the two parties to settle the dispute through negotiations.

The United Kingdom was forced out of comfortable inaction, certainly a logical stance to have taken, inasmuch as it enjoyed the possession and use of the islands. In January 1966, Sir Michael Stewart, secretary of foreign relations, traveled to Buenos Aires as the first high-level Foreign Office official to visit Argentina. Meetings were cordial, and the British were unusually receptive to Argentina's firm claim. Argentina would insist on it once again in London, formally setting out its rights in a note that July. As a consequence, the first bilateral meeting on the Malvinas question took place.

Beck, whose excellent and well-documented work I cite frequently throughout this chapter, says that Stewart's visit in January of 1966 "prepared the ground for the initiation of bilateral exchanges in pursuit of a modus vivendi on the future of the islands." He adds that this step basically reflected the ongoing transformation in British foreign policy according to which the future of the Falklands was reevaluated in a changing domestic and international context. (S. 21, p. 97)

Beck enumerates some of the factors contributing to this new context: fiscal austerity measures taken on February 22, 1966; the emphasis on a European rather than worldwide role; the permanent retreat of the empire; and the advent of a Labour government that was anticolonial and eager for better relations with Latin America. Beck also cites the negotiating climate brought about by the signing of the Antarctic Treaty as indicative that both countries "were capable of rational discussions." (Ibid., p. 98)

Consequently, as Professor Metford notes in a somewhat critical vein, the Malvinas were "no longer important . . . and therefore scarcely worth retaining," especially in view of the difficulty of defending one of the most remote borders of an empire in decline (S. 28, p. 479).

The beginning of bilateral negotiations: The possibility of transfer of sovereignty is outlined. Returning to our strongest British source, the Franks Report notes that after the secret discussions of July 1966, others were conducted in November 1966 and February 1967. In Argentina a military coup had placed General J. C. Onganía at the head of a de facto government, but the steadfastness of the Foreign Ministry on this issue did not diminish under his designate, Nicanor Costa Méndez. And the pressure must have been considerable for George Brown, secretary of state for foreign affairs, and Fred Lee, secretary of state for the colonies, to have thought at the time that Argentina could easily take the islands by force. The Franks Report tells us that "at the talks the British side initially proposed a sovereignty freeze for a minimum of 30 years. . . . At the end of this period the Islanders would be free to choose between British and Argentine rule" (S. 1, p. 5).

The Argentine government rejected this proposal, and the Franks Report acknowledges that "in March 1967 the British government for the first time stated formally to Argentina that they would be prepared to cede sovereignty over the islands under certain conditions" (Ibid.). This is the same conclusive statement quoted earlier from the Kershaw Report, which, according to Beck, "reflected the 'active' approach towards foreign affairs advocated by George Brown, Foreign Secretary from 1965 to 1968" (S. 21, p. 99).

The official British source I am using states that negotiations were underway to agree on the text for future reference, which would be called a Memorandum of Understanding. The Franks Report adds that in early 1968 the governor of the islands showed the Executive Council of the islands a confidential preliminary version of the memorandum. As a result, on February 27 unofficial members of the council sent an Open Letter to the members of Parliament alerting them to negotiations "which may result at any moment in the handing over of the Falklands to the Argentine" (S. 1, p. 6).

When Michael Stewart returned to the Foreign Office in 1968 to replace George Brown, a situation was already developing as a consequence of pockets of opposition to the understanding. This made him clarify that any transfer of sovereignty would have to be part of an agreement that would ensure a permanently satisfactory relationship between Argentina and the islands, "where there should be no harassing, no vexation, no inconvenience." If there were to be a transfer of sovereignty, there should be a complete safeguarding of the essential rights of the Islanders, and the transfer itself would take place "only if it were clear to us . . . that the Islanders themselves regarded such an agreement as satisfactory to their interests." (Ibid.) The language is subtle, but it is clear that the government retained the opinion of the population as a key element.

Franks adds that in March 1969 the pressure against a transfer of sovereignty increased so much that the government was considering restrictions on its freedom of action, even before the Memorandum of

Understanding had been agreed upon by the parties. He also comments that, because of strong protests in Parliament and in the press, Mr. Stewart and other ministers of the Foreign Office had to state for the record on several occasions that "there would be no cession of sovereignty against the wishes of the Islanders" (S. 1, p. 6).

Beck identifies three pockets of opposition, which he analyzes in detail in his work: (1) the Islanders (organized as the FIEC, the Falkland Islands Executive Council); (2) the press; and (3) Parliament. In any case, what must be remembered is that the British government began to let its hands be tied, and the bonds, represented by these three sectors, tightened more each time a decision was to be made.

The agreement on the Memorandum of Understanding. Beck is of the opinion that Stewart, in spite of the pressure, continued favoring a formula that would preserve the interests of the Islanders—and not their "desires"—so that in the future they would be able to live on good terms with their neighbors. He believed in the advantage of ensuring a more stable relationship, which would facilitate communication between the Islanders and Argentina and would benefit the United Kingdom's position in Latin America and in the United Nations. (S. 21, p. 101)

Endowed with a statesman's keen vision, capable of looking beyond his own political clout in spite of the negative climate described, Stewart continued negotiating with the Argentines. On March 28, Beck says, he informed the cabinet of the formula proposed for submission. Finally, in August 1968—as Lord Franks writes—agreement was reached on a text entitled Memorandum of Understanding.

The Franks Report made this important document public—15 years after the fact. In the "crucial part on sovereignty," as it was called, the report reads as follows:

> The government of the United Kingdom as part of such final settlement will recognize Argentina's sovereignty over the islands from a date to be agreed. This date will be agreed as soon as possible after: (i) the two governments have resolved the present divergence between them as to the criteria according to which the United Kingdom Government shall consider whether the interest of the Islanders would be secured by the safeguards and guarantees to be offered by the Argentine government, and (ii) the Government of the United Kingdom are then satisfied that those interests are so secured. (S. 1, p. 6)

The report continues, saying that the publication of the memorandum should be accompanied by a unilateral declaration in which it is made clear that the government was willing to proceed to a definitive arrangement with Argentina that would include transfer of sovereignty only when it was satisfied that the transfer and the basis on which it would take place were acceptable to the population of the islands. (Ibid.)

Beck, with the advantage of a meticulous survey of British archives, comments on this document—an authentic pearl of bilateral negotiation— with these words:

> In August 1968 Anglo-Argentine exchanges culminated in an agreed text of the Memorandum, according to which the government of the United Kingdom as part of a final settlement will recognize Argentina's sovereignty over the islands from a date to be agreed. Argentine sovereignty would be acknowledged after four and within ten years while the date would be settled when the British government was satisfied that "the interests of the Islanders" were secured and guaranteed. (S. 21, p. 101)

In spite of the complicated scenario, the document that was agreed to—and here one must pay tribute to the Argentine negotiators—certainly laid the foundations for restitution of the Malvinas to their legitimate owners within a short period of time.

Rejection by Parliament: The United Kingdom puts aside the subject of sovereignty. The text remained secret as to its exact terms—at least this was surely the wish of the Foreign Office—but as Beck points out, the active Malvinas lobby began to close off possibilities for negotiation.

Even when the memorandum's prospects were diminishing, Lord Chalfont, the minister of state in charge of negotiations, visited the islands to explain the latest political developments.

Beck maintains that the Islanders were not impressed by the first ministerial visit and the lobby again reacted strongly: Some 100 parliamentarians signed a motion requiring the British government "once and for all to assert that the Falkland Islanders are British and would not be transferred against their will to an alien land" (S. 21, p. 102).

Beck relates that after passing through Buenos Aires and finding what he termed the same lack of flexibility, Lord Chalfont informed Stewart of this "conflict of 'irreconcilables'; unless sovereignty is seriously negotiated, and ceded in the long term, we are likely to end up in armed conflict with Argentina," which, Beck adds, was considered unduly alarming. (Ibid.)

As to these events, the Franks Report says that the government made statements regarding this visit before both Houses of Parliament on December 3, 1968, which met with criticism and were widely quoted in the press (S. 1, p. 6). Beck completes this bit of information with what happened in a cabinet meeting held on December 5 in which those present "noting that it had 'blown up into a great issue in Parliament' concluded that 'the whole thing is off'" (Ibid., p. 103).

I have meticulously reviewed the dramatic development of this proposal in order to present the clearest view of the other side of the story, as told by an irreproachable British source, regarding the negotiations on the Malvinas question. The epilogue to the most genuine Argentine expectation to accede to sovereignty over the islands was imminent and—as became clear—would prove contrary to this hope. With the doors of Parliament once again closed, the representatives of its constituency could not come to the support of this objective. Nor could Argentine diplomacy—successful at the negotiating table—count on a democratic country's mobilization of the international community in favor of its just cause.

In fact, as the Franks Report emphasizes, given pressure in Parliament and the reaction from the press, "the Government decided at a Cabinet meeting on 11 December not to continue to attempt to reach a settlement on the basis of the Memorandum of Understanding" (S. 1, p. 7).

The official report commented upon claims to imply, ingenuously in my opinion, that the fault was Argentina's, adding:

> Since Argentina was not prepared to accept either that the Memorandum should include a statement that any transfer of sovereignty would be subject to the wishes of the Islanders; or that the unilateral statement, enshrining this safeguard, should be specifically linked to the Memorandum. (Ibid.)

It is very clear from a reading of the British report itself that this last assessment is not correct. What happened was that, mainly due to domestic politics, the United Kingdom had modified its original approach. In its new approach it replaced respect for the Islanders' "interests" with respect for their "wishes," thereby submitting the entire agreement to a veto by the people of the islands.

It remains to be shown that Stewart, that same evening, made a statement in Parliament saying that negotiations with Argentina would continue but that the British would insist on the "paramountcy of the Islanders' wishes" (S. 1, p. 7).

In this manner, what had been the most promising stage of bilateral negotiations was aborted. Although—as we shall soon see—there were other significant proposals, apparently they never were based on the political will that had motivated several British officials at high political levels, including two who headed the Foreign Office, Michael Stewart and George Brown.

What is clear is that with the Memorandum of Understanding rejected, the British government demonstrated its willingness to continue the negotiations—but with a totally different approach. As Beck says:

> Therefore sovereignty, which had been in the forefront during 1966–1968 was pushed aside and the disputants were forced to concentrate upon more practical issues, like communications, under the "sovereignty

umbrella"—that is without prejudice to their respective legal positions. (S. 21, p. 104)

The position of the lobby favoring the status quo had been imposed and the principle of self-determination was granted supremacy, in its larger interpretation (S. 21, p. 104). Consequently, "the Islanders' interests were elevated to wishes as the paramount condition" in any solution on the future of the Islands" (Ibid.).

An evaluation of this failure: Its causes and effects. I have just analyzed one of the most important moments in the diplomatic struggle to recover the Malvinas Islands, the one, perhaps, at which the two sides came closest to an agreement that fundamentally considered the rights of the Argentine Republic. As Beck says, this was when "the handover of the islands seemed imminent" (S. 9, p. 42) and the influence of the Islanders had been correctly placed in perspective, without giving them veto power.

It is also the episode that most clearly demonstrates the validity of Argentina's title. No country in the world would have been willing to transfer sovereignty over part of its territory without being fully convinced of the rights of the party claiming it.

Development of the facts clearly shows the factors frustrating the negotiating exercise on the part of both foreign ministries. Nonetheless, given its importance and at the risk of appearing repetitious, I shall summarize the causes in two broad categories:

The poor handling of the matter politically. According to Beck, there was hastiness and a lack of prudence. Neither the Islanders nor the press were fully informed "about the merits of an agreed accommodation with Argentina." As a result, because of misinformation and strong emotions, a feeling was created "that the Islanders were being sacrificed on the altar of Anglo-Argentine relations." (Ibid., p. 106)

It is inescapable that the Labour government displayed a lack of preparation and did not give Stewart sufficient support showing a tendency to follow rather than lead public opinion and politics (Ibid.). From one point of view, it can be argued that the Malvinas question was transformed from an international problem into a priority domestic matter, in which confusion overcame the very parties involved in the dispute over sovereignty.

The solid articulation of interests favorable to the status quo. As Beck says, the Falkland Islands lobby obtained support in all political parties and made enough noise to start up, in a peripheral matter, what is called the "voice of Parliament," thereby complicating the ministers' position and obtaining press coverage (Ibid.).

On the other hand, there was no lobby in favor of the Argentine position—or, rather, the Latin American position—and only a few members of the Labour Party defended the understanding as responding to broader British interests at stake and to anticolonialism. Again Beck points out the strong support for the islands lobby, which contrasted "with the relative lack of support for Stewart within and outside Parliament" (Ibid., p. 105).

In conclusion, seen in its historical perspective, this episode takes on even more dramatic overtones. More than a few British writers emphasize the importance of 1968 to the conflict of 1982. Beck states it in these words: "Argentina had seen the door to the Malvinas, and possibly beyond towards South Georgia, the South Sandwich Islands and Antarctica, opened suddenly after being tightly closed for over a century, and then shut again" (Ibid.).

But, above all, the interests that advocated "keep the Falklands British" had joined forces and had successfully shown their strength. They would never again abandon their militant attitude, and their militancy contrasted with the indifference British economic interests linked to Argentina had always shown toward the Malvinas question. Unfortunately, their Argentine associates in Buenos Aires showed the same indifference. With a few honorable exceptions, they had always proved more concerned with their stock in the "City" than with the future of the rocky southern archipelagoes.

I must emphasize the last point for two reasons. First, because, truthfully, that is the conclusion I reached in the period during which I was responsible for handling the matter. And in the second place because I am convinced that this attitude will have to change if Argentines still aspire to see their flag fly again over the territories in dispute.

The condominium proposal.

The interregnum: The communications policy. The British, after the frustrating negotiating exercise related above, demonstrated their willingness to continue discussions, but limited them to aspects that were more pragmatic and less controversial. They claimed the political scenario had become very sensitized to the subject and indicated the necessity for a more benevolent vision of Argentina on the part of the Islanders. It would therefore be appropriate to initiate a policy of contacts and communication between the islands and continental Argentina.

This third diplomatic procedure—in addition to the multilateral and bilateral I have described—began in early 1969, and at the end of that year both parties communicated to the United Nations the initiation of discussions directed toward that goal.

This limited approach—a true interregnum in the negotiation of sovereignty—was accentuated in 1970 with the arrival of the Conservative government of Edward Heath to power. The following year, in August 1971, both parties approved in an exchange of notes three documents previously negotiated in London and Buenos Aires. Among them was a joint declaration putting into place a series of initiatives, of which one of the most significant was the construction of a temporary landing field by the Argentine Air Force. It was completed in November 1972.

But with the advent of the Justicialista government in Argentina in May 1973, there was strongly increased pressure to resume negotiations over sovereignty, cornering the United Kingdom, which tried to evade the subject. As the Franks Report states—as a logical consequence of this different view of the matter—"it became clear that an impasse had been reached" (S. 1, p. 8).

Argentine pressure: The formalization of a condominium proposal. As it has traditionally done when it wants to corner the British and sit them down to negotiate the subject central to the dispute, the Argentine government turned to the United Nations. On December 14, 1973, the General Assembly adopted Resolution 3160 (XXVIII). It expressed serious concern for the lack of progress in the negotiations and called on both parties to accelerate them with a view toward a solution to the sovereignty dispute and, it added, with the goal of putting an end to the colonial situation. This must be emphasized because there was no suggestion that the solution would perpetuate British dominion, as the British have sometimes rather insolently maintained at the negotiating table.

In view of the pressure from the United Nations and the risk, the Franks Report says, of an economic and military offensive against the islands, in January 1974 the Defence Committee "agreed that the likely attitude of the Islanders to the possibility of condominium as an alternative to a transfer of sovereignty should be discussed with the Governor of the Falkland Islands." Both he and the British ambassador in Buenos Aires advised that "the idea was worth pursuing." (S. 1, p. 8)

Before this initiative could be put into practice, however, the general election of March 1974 again installed the Labour Party in power with Harold Wilson as prime minister and James Callaghan as head of the Foreign Office.

The new government, called upon to choose from among a series of options on the Malvinas question, "decided in the Defence Committee to consult the Falkland Islands Executive Council on the possibility of initiating talks with Argentina on condominium. . . . The Council indicated that it would raise no objection to talk on condominium . . . provided that there was no Islander participation initially" (S. 1, p. 8).

It should be noted that for the United Kingdom, consultation regarding the Islanders' willingness has acquired the characteristic of a necessary step in the negotiating process with Argentina. The latter has always rejected this attitude, permanently refusing to accept a sort of third party in the dispute over sovereignty.

Thus, with the approval of the population of the islands, the Argentine government was officially informed for the first time of the proposal for condominium. The Franks Report confirms this, saying: "The subject of condominium was broached with the Argentine government" (S. 1, p. 8).

It is interesting to note that in June 1974, the British ambassador in Buenos Aires received instructions to resume discussions on the future of the Malvinas "on the basis of the safeguards and guarantees to be extended to the Islanders in the hypothetical event of a condominium," without prejudice to their respective positions on sovereignty. The initiative sent to the Argentine Foreign Ministry explained that "the main aim of Her Majesty's government in entering into negotiations on the basis of a condominium would be to settle the dispute about sovereignty by accepting Argentina's co-sovereignty over the islands." It added that it had to be consolidated by a treaty "creating a favorable atmosphere in which the Islanders could develop according to their interests."

The note (which I reviewed through a private source in Argentina) concluded with an important paragraph stating that "a Joint Session of the Executive and Legislative Councils of the islands have informed the Governor that they have no objection to talks being held with the Argentine Government on the safeguards and guarantees required in a condominium." It clarified that Islanders could be among the British delegation and that before final agreement the Islanders would be formally consulted and their acceptance sought by some form of popular representation.

Some accounts question whether Foreign Minister Vignes had analyzed this proposal with the recently reelected president, Juan Domingo Perón, or whether there was ever a response from the Argentine government rejecting the terms or requesting greater detail. What is important in this essay is what the British admit, and the Franks Report says, "But in the face of the Islanders' continuing refusal to participate, it was decided that there would be no purpose in proceeding without them, and the Argentine Government were so informed in August 1974" (S. 1, p. 8).

It is appropriate to stress the weight that the Labour administration also granted to the will of the people of the islands, given that their sole failure to cooperate in the proposal—not because of active obstruction but by simple omission—proved to be its downfall.

Thus, once again because of the Islanders' attitude, another proposal was discarded. A month later, in spite of this step backwards, Argentina still maintained its constructive attitude and was advancing in economic accords, with a grant to Yacimientos Petrolíferos Fiscales (the state-run oil company) to supply petroleum products to the islands. This was effected at prices very advantageous to the Islanders.

Condominium reappears among Conservative options (1979–1980). The 1974 events I have related constitute the clearest case of a proposal of condominium within the framework of negotiations on the sovereignty dispute. It is appropriate to note here that although Foreign Minister Owen had considered different ways of sharing sovereignty, Prime Minister Callaghan after the 1974 failure did not lend his support to the condominium idea, at least not as a solution for the Malvinas Islands.

Five years would pass before condominium would again surface among the options the Foreign Office bandied about in its proposals submitted after 1979 to the Conservative administration of Margaret Thatcher. There is evidence that it was on the slate offered to the population of the islands in early 1980 when Secretary of State Nicholas Ridley, named by the new administration as chief of the negotiations, visited the Malvinas.

Let us see how Mr. Hunt, the former governor and then British commissioner in the islands, describes this visit when questioned by Lord Kershaw in 1983: Ridley, during his visit in 1980, had several meetings in Stanley and also toured the camp and spoke with the council members "to explain the three options that he had been able to think about with the advice of his officials. Those three options were a (1) freeze, (2) a leaseback or (3) a condominium. At a Legislative Council session the Councilors debated it and came up with a resolution saying they could not see a condominium as being a starter" (S. 3, p. 193).

This means the Conservatives reintroduced condominium among the range of options on several occasions, although they always demonstrated a preference for another scheme—leaseback—to which I will refer later. As the Kershaw Committee says:

> In the process several compromise proposals—all ultimately unsatisfactory to at least one of the parties involved—were tried out by the British Government on both the Argentine Government and the Falklands Legislative Council. The most important of these were the possibility of a shared administration (or condominium) and the possibility of a leaseback arrangement, under which both Argentine sovereignty and British administration could simultaneously be recognised. (S. 6, p. xix)

Both options, leaseback and condominium, involved recognition of Argentine sovereignty. We must therefore again pose the question: Would Great Britain have been willing to contemplate such options had it in fact had no doubts as to its own title? I think not. Again, the other party's confession is the best proof of Argentina's case.

The new terms of reference for bilateral negotiations: Sovereignty and economic cooperation.

British interest in the joint exploitation of resources. Let us again take up the thread connecting these events. The proposal for condominium was abandoned in August 1974, and although the policy of communications with the islands continued to evolve, the British came up with nothing new on the question of sovereignty. This certainly did not satisfy General Perón's government, which was under increased pressure to show progress on that front.

Argentina's persistence and the perception by the United Kingdom, according to Franks, that Argentina might be formulating contingency plans to invade the islands, prompted an evaluation by the Joint Committee on British Intelligence. It concluded that military action was improbable "as long as Argentina believed that the British Government were prepared to negotiate sovereignty" (S. 1, p. 9).

The message could not be more clear: It was not necessary to negotiate sovereignty over the islands; it was sufficient for Argentina to believe that to be the case. I draw attention to this situation because as time went by, the United Kingdom's tendency to misrepresent its true political will became more acute. In the opinion of some specialists in the field, therein lies a major cause of the dramatic events of 1982.

As a consequence of the Joint Committee's evaluation and the perceived need to show progress in negotiations, a proposal was considered that included the joint exercise of jurisdiction over natural resources. In this connection the Franks Report says: "The next British initiative was a proposal, approved by the Defence Committee in July 1975, for discussions of joint Anglo-Argentine development of the resources of the Southwest Atlantic" (Ibid.).

The report quoted continues, commenting on the Argentine reaction: "In response to this proposal, Mr. Vignes suggested linking such initiative to the possibility of transfer of sovereignty followed by simultaneous leaseback for a period of years, as a means of settling the dispute." He proposed moreover that Great Britain accept immediate Argentine occupation of the South Georgias and the South Sandwich Islands. It was a daring suggestion that caught the British off-guard. Franks says that "Vignes was warned that any such unilateral action would be quite unacceptable." (Ibid., p. 9)

Argentina, for its part, rejected negotiations limited to economic cooperation, on the grounds that they excluded the subject of sovereignty.

Events move quickly: The Shackleton Mission and the deterioration of bilateral relations. In October 1975, the British government, on the basis of its revived interest in the renewable and nonrenewable resources of the area—let us not forget the energy crisis of 1973 and the lack of information on the extent of deposits in the North Sea—commissioned Lord Shackleton to do a study of these resources for the long term in order to identify actions that could improve the economy of the islands.

The Argentine Foreign Ministry made public its displeasure in a communiqué saying that this was an "unwelcome initiative to which Argentina has not agreed" (Ibid., p. 9). Nonetheless, the journey took place in early January 1976, prompting a harsh note from the Argentine Foreign Ministry. It pointed out the fact that the British had broken off negotiations, that this increased the risks of conflict, and that the United Kingdom would be responsible for such a disastrous result. Lord Shackleton's report appeared in May of the same year.

Let us follow, through the British source cited, the evolution of the events that led to a serious deterioration in bilateral relations.

On January 12, 1976, an answer from Callaghan purporting to be conciliatory and in which the sovereignty dispute was termed "sterile" drew a reply from Argentina the following day, pointing out that this reference was insulting and complaining of the lack of positive elements to reopen the negotiations on sovereignty. A press communiqué announced the same day that the Argentine government had decided not to send their ambassador back to London and "to suggest" that the British ambassador in Buenos Aires should be withdrawn (Ibid., p. 10).

On January 14, 1976, Foreign Minister Callaghan made a statement in the House of Commons that managed to calm anxieties. However, the cost of fortifying the islands because of renewed pressure by Argentina was carefully calculated.

On February 11, 1976, Secretary of State Ted Rowlands, appointed by Labour, traveled to new York to meet with the new Argentine Foreign Minister, Ambassador Raúl Quijano. At the meeting, he suggested that Argentina should make the proposals it wanted to discuss on the subject of sovereignty, clarifying that "the British government would defend the islands if the Argentines attempted to use force" (Ibid., p. 12).

In March 1976, given the deterioration of relations and observing an agreement in principle reached in the New York meeting, Minister Callaghan decided "to undertake a major review of policy. The same month, the Cabinet approved his proposal for a fresh dialogue on all aspects of the dispute, both the possibility of Anglo-Argentine economic cooperation in the Southwest Atlantic and . . . the nature of a hypothetical future constitutional relationship" (Ibid., p. 13). This decision was communicated in a note to the Argentine government.

In December 1976, Argentine diplomats again turned to the United Nations, which adopted the now classic Resolution calling for a solution to the sovereignty dispute through bilateral negotiation. Resolution 31/49 (according to the new numbering system) introduced a dispositive paragraph establishing, for the first time in the history of the Malvinas question, the principle of noninnovation. Because of this—and also because of a paragraph in the preamble referring to a decision by the Non-Aligned Movement that recognized Argentine sovereignty—the United Kingdom voted against the Resolution.

The discovery of an Argentine scientific station in South Thule (South Sandwich) the previous summer evoked a British protest in January 1977.

The negotiating mandate of April 1977: The sovereignty dispute extends to the three southern archipelagoes. The British message of March 1976 launching a new dialogue was not successful—perhaps because of the overthrow of Isabel Perón's government at the end of the month—but when James Callaghan was promoted to prime minister, he continued his project.

On February 2, 1977, a statement in Parliament by Minister Crossland "announced the Government's decision that the time has come to consider both with the Islanders and the Argentine Government whether a climate exists for discussing the broad issues which bear on the future of the Falkland Islands and the possibilities of cooperation between Britain and Argentina in the region of the Southwest Atlantic." The report adds:

> He made it clear that in any discussions the Government would reserve their position on sovereignty; that any changes which might be proposed must be acceptable to the Islanders; and that there must be full consultation with the Islanders at every stage. (Ibid., p. 15)

The Defence Committee approved a visit to the islands by Rowlands and also indicated that he should maintain discussions in Buenos Aires. The visit occurred in February 1977, and after intensive meetings, the Island Council cooperated in drafting the terms of reference—see below—which were always to be under a "sovereignty umbrella."

After Rowlands's discussions in Buenos Aires—secret, as had been another previous meeting in Rome—the terms of the mandate for negotiation were agreed upon and were set forth in a joint communiqué dated April 26, the date it was released in both capitals. The text of this document, which David Owen, the brand-new foreign minister, announced in the Chamber of Commons the following day can be summarized as follows:

- It dealt with two broad subjects:
  i. future political relations, including sovereignty over the Malvinas Islands, the South Georgias, and the South Sandwich Islands; and
  ii. economic cooperation in these territories in particular and in the South Atlantic in general.
- It defined as the purposes of the negotiations the formulation of a peaceful solution to the sovereignty dispute existing between the two states and the establishment of a framework for Anglo-Argentine economic cooperation that would substantially contribute to the development of the islands and of the region in general.

- It affirmed that another object of the negotiations was to achieve a stable, prosperous, and politically durable future for the islands, whose people the government of the United Kingdom would consult during the course of the negotiations.
- It placed the agreement to hold negotiations, and the negotiations themselves, under a "sovereignty umbrella," that is, they would not prejudice the position of either government with regard to sovereignty over the islands.

The last paragraph of these terms of reference for the bilateral negotiations concluded with practical considerations: The level, the time, and the place of the meetings would be determined by mutual agreement between the parties, as would the constitution of working groups if necessary (see Appendix 3).

It is clear that the April 1977 mandate could not be invoked in an international court of justice or in arbitration because a reservation on sovereignty—the famous "umbrella"—was placed in the text itself protecting the substantive position of the parties. But it is quite clear that both parties were willing to include in the discussions the questions of

- sovereignty over the territory of the three southern archipelagoes to which for the first time it expressly refers; and
- the economic resources of these territories, and those corresponding to the jurisdiction recognized by international law as belonging to the coastal state.

The mixed approach: Concessions in the uninhabited islands.

Political smoke screen and economic interest. Analyzed today from a historical perspective, the strategy of the United Kingdom reflected in the terms of reference of April 1977 is clear: Interest demonstrated in 1975 in progressing toward cooperation with Argentina in the exploitation of the natural resources in the area was still alive, but to obtain it the United Kingdom had to at least appear willing to make concessions. That is, given the reasons for rejection of the proposal of July of that year, it had to be sweetened with the inclusion of the sovereignty issue.

The Franks Report, using different words, admits this: "Broadly speaking, the Government's strategy was to retain sovereignty as long as possible, if necessary making concessions in respect of the Dependencies (Georgia and Sandwich) and the maritime resources in the area" (S. 1, p. 17). This then, was the strategy. It is interesting now to state precisely in what manner and to what extent it was put into practice, that is, proposed to and negotiated with Argentina.

There are few British sources on this period that cover 1978, but the Franks report says that discussions went reasonably well and options were kept open. It adds: "The British side put forward the idea that the sovereignty of the uninhabited dependencies might be looked at separately from the sovereignty of the Falkland Islands themselves" (S. 1, p. 17).

Beck, in his latest work, also sheds a little more light on this stage:

> The British government, realising the difficulty of progress on Falklands sovereignty, interpreted the possibility of concessions on either regional, economic and scientific cooperation, or the sovereignty of the FID (T.N., Falkland Islands Dependencies) [there was no indigenous population to complicate the issue] as methods of keeping the line open to Buenos Aires. (S. 21, pp. 119–120)

And he concludes that the Malvinas Islands and their "Dependencies"—FID in British administrative jargon, that is, the South Georgias and the South Sandwich Islands—heretofore separate from the dispute, "became increasingly intertwined" (Ibid., p. 117).

We see that British sources recognize—that is, they admit—that the British government put forward an initiative that distinguished sovereignty over the Malvinas from sovereignty over the "Dependencies"—their case was less complicated because they were uninhabited islands—and that regarding both the sovereignty over these archipelagoes and the resources of the entire area, they were ready to make concessions.

The "Rowlands paper." The paragraphs quoted from the Franks Report and by Peter Beck reveal only the essence of a proposal that a British delegation presented at the meeting held in New York on December 13, 1977. At that time, a working paper from Mr. Rowlands was delivered that contained a series of elements as the general framework for the negotiations.

In this informal document, the Labour administration identified several criteria. Among them is one mentioned in the Franks Report concerning the differentiation between the territories according to whether or not they were inhabited. The paper calls this basic criterion a "mixed approach." Moreover, it emphasized the necessity of obtaining a balance between Argentina's essential interest in the territory of the Malvinas and the essential concern of the British for sovereign rights in relation to the people. The remaining criteria referred to maintaining the Islanders' existing way of life, to providing a framework that would permit economic improvement in their standard of living, and to developing the major resources of the area, the latter by resolving the dispute that had been an obstacle to achieving this.

The paper likewise identified the three physical components of the negotiations: (1) The Malvinas Islands—with both territory and people; (2) the Dependencies (included in the terms of reference of April 1977), which were territories with no resident population; and (3) an element with its own peculiarities, the ocean and the continental shelf.

The most substantive portion of the paper was where ideas were put forward as to the characteristics of the negotiations. It began by referring to the Dependencies and their maritime zones, perhaps because they were less controversial, over which the British government was willing to consider some new sovereignty arrangements in favor of Argentina. It added that to the extent the new sovereignty arrangements included the maritime zones, they should reflect the real interests of the two countries and ensure controlled use of resources, to which access by third parties should be regulated.

The working document later referred to the Malvinas Islands and its maritime areas, and emphasized the paramount concern of the British government for the inhabitants, and concern that sovereign rights over them should remain with the United Kingdom. As for the maritime areas (maritime resources and those of the continental shelf), special arrangements should produce a framework for economic activity beneficial to all parties concerned, as both governments had stipulated.

It was an initiative rich in possibilities—as there was no lack of sovereignty arrangements of every type—and obviously it generated high expectations in the Argentine Foreign Ministry. The facts would demonstrate that it was more of a negotiating tactic than a demonstration of authentic political will to progress toward real concessions.

The draft report of the Foreign Affairs Committee of the House of Commons records it precisely as a negotiating tactic. In referring to the Dependencies in paragraph 6.6, it recognizes that the idea that the South Georgias and the South Sandwich Islands might contribute to an arrangement with Argentina had been bandied about on several occasions. And it adds:

> However, their usefulness as a bargaining card does not appear clear. It has been argued by those who believe that the true economic potential of the region lies to the south and in the Antarctica that British sovereignty over the Falkland Islands might be traded off for an Argentine recognition of British sovereignty over the Dependencies. The converse possibility has also been raised. (S. 4, p. xlvii)

Now that we are familiar with the initiatives, let us see how discussions evolved. As was noted in February 1978 in New York, two working groups met in Lima, one on sovereignty and the other on economic cooperation.

In Lima there was an impasse, which led to an informal meeting of high-level officials in New York toward mid-September 1978. Its goal was to unblock the negotiations and prepare for the traditional meeting of foreign affairs ministers, which was to coincide with the United Nations General Assembly.

During the course of the meeting, Ambassador George Hall illustrated several aspects of the Rowlands paper. He said that it probably contemplated joint administration of the maritime areas, which assumed a joint declaration on a 200-mile limit and the following practical measures: licensing, exercise of police power, exploitation of resources, and so forth. He likewise clarified that the mixed approach meant different solutions to the three issues in dispute—that is, the maritime areas and the territories, inhabited or uninhabited.

Finally, he interpreted any sovereignty arrangement over the uninhabited territories as linked to the ideas referring to a solution for the Malvinas, recognizing that this issue was the most complex.

Ah treacherous Albion! With this simple tactic—almost a dialectic game—the British side contrived a grant of priority to its own interests: that is, the arrangements conducive to the exploitation of resources, beginning with the maritime areas of the South Georgias and the South Sandwich Islands. Any decision on sovereignty over any territory involved in the negotiation was postponed, which affected the "rule of proportionality" established by Argentina with respect to substantive advances.

In any event, none of this was beyond the intent of the Labour Party, which the realities of British domestic politics rapidly left in a dubious position.

Labour's failure:
Draft Agreement on Scientific Cooperation
and its rejection by the Islanders.

After the meeting described and another in New York involving both foreign ministers, the impasse ended and a new round of negotiations in Geneva was planned for December 1978. The British had reduced the material to be negotiated, and after suggesting the possibility of an accord on cooperation in the exploitation of resources in the Dependencies, they proposed beginning with one limited to scientific cooperation, the bases for which would be negotiated in the round held in the vicinity of Lake Geneva. The Franks Report recounts this meeting as follows:

> There were no more formal negotiations [if the New York meeting could be called formal] until, following Argentine agreement to discuss maritime zones and shelf rights within negotiations, a meeting at the ministerial level was held in December of 1979 in Geneva. Agreement in principle was reached on a draft cooperation agreement on scientific activities in the Dependencies. (S. 1, p. 19)

Meanwhile, the Argentine Foreign Ministry was pressuring for a more dynamic sequence in the bilateral meetings. Given that the negotiating scheme also contemplated meetings of high-level officials—in addition to those involving ministers—one was held in New York in early March 1979. There, the Labour government, perhaps convinced of its imminent departure from power—the election took place the same month—took a particularly negative position, through Undersecretary George Hall, its intermediary, who announced that, "owing to the Falkland Islanders' suspicions of the motives of the Argentine Government, it was not possible to sign the agreement on scientific cooperation" (Ibid., p. 19).

Once again, as with the Memorandum of Understanding, the Islanders' lobby favoring the status quo dashed the hopes of negotiators from both countries. This assessment is shared by the Franks Report. In point 70 under the title "Significant Themes of the Period 1965–1979," it says:

> i. Successive British governments sought a solution to the Falkland Islands dispute by negotiation; and they recognised that any solution negotiated with Argentina had to be acceptable to the Islanders.
>
> ii. The negotiating options gradually narrowed. The Labour government made clear in 1977 that sovereignty was an issue for negotiation.

And it adds:

> But, although transfer of sovereignty combined with leaseback had come to be regarded by the British government as the most realistic solution, the leaseback proposal was not discussed with Argentina during this period. (S. 1, p. 19)

Foreign Minister Owen did not particularly favor the leaseback scheme—which I will analyze shortly—but if this approach to the territory of the Malvinas had been included in the Rowlands paper, it would have been a good basis for progress. It constituted a constructive and imaginative scheme allowing both governments to work toward obtaining economic benefits for all the parties concerned. As the paper said, those ideas offered the opportunity not only to resolve a dispute of a hundred years duration, but also in doing so to create a prosperous and stable future for everyone living in the area. Moreover, it would probably have modified the Islanders' own perception of the fruits of a close relationship with Argentina and would have forestalled the dramatic events that both peoples were to experience some three years later.

It is undeniable that the initiatives to which I have referred constitute another major example of an implicit British recognition of Argentine rights over both the three southern archipelagoes and their corresponding maritime areas.

Transfer of sovereignty with a leaseback
to the United Kingdom.

Description and background of the proposal. This subchapter refers to a proposal that was actively considered by successive British administrations as the most possible and most realistic solution to the institutional future of the Malvinas Islands. Modeled basically on the relationship the United Kingdom has with China with respect to the colony of Hong Kong, it consists essentially of a transfer of sovereignty to a country claiming the territory, subject to an agreed-upon deferral during which the former administration remains in office as a lessee enjoying the rights of the new holder of sovereignty.

According to the Franks Report, the earliest mention of this scheme dates back to June 1975 and came from Argentina. This must have occurred during the Justicialista administration which, through Foreign Minister Vignes, proposed it as part of the sine qua non for the British initiative of that period regarding joint development of the resources of the area (S. 1, p. 9). As we saw, at that time it was rejected by the United Kingdom.

In the preceding paragraph, it is inferred that a proposal of this type was not unknown to the Labour administration, after negotiations acquired a more dynamic rhythm with the terms of reference agreed upon in April 1977. The Franks Report reveals to us the subtleties of the policy of this period:

Before the first round of talks Dr. Owen presented a paper to the Defence Committee in July 1977, which argued that serious and substantive negotiations were necessary

> to keep the Argentines in play, since the islands were indefensible except by a major, costly and unacceptable diversion of current resources. . . .
> The Committee took the view that it was likely that the government would be forced back in the end on some variation of a leaseback solution linked with a programme of joint economic cooperation. (S. 1, p. 17)

In other words, aware of the necessity for change, the Labour Party adopted the strategy of maintaining substantive negotiations with Argentina. And, without prejudice to other sovereignty arrangements in the uninhabited islands and over resources—with an accent on the latter according to what we have just seen—they viewed the leaseback as a scheme that eventually they would have to accept in order to resolve the dispute over the Malvinas territories.

Commenting critically on the Franks Report, W. Wallace, another British writer, confirmed that Rowlands "was able to avoid proposing leaseback during the discussions" and in spite of having been considered the most realistic proposal, "the leaseback proposal was not discussed with Argentina" (S. 12, p. 455).

It is clear to me that this statement is correct, although according to Beck during 1978 and 1979: "The British government was prepared, at least in private, to contemplate the transfer of sovereignty, possibly combined with leaseback over a period of 70 years" (S. 21, p. 119). Beck even tells us the number of years (70) that the United Kingdom thought of prolonging British administration.

In summary, during the Labour administration, although the mandate was excellent, the little that was negotiated in two years was based on ideas contained in the Rowlands paper and without the United Kingdom's formal suggestion of solution based on the formula applied in Hong Kong.

Preference for this proposal at the beginning of the current Conservative administration. Initial contacts with the Conservative government of Margaret Thatcher were cordial, in a climate forged in the decision to reestablish diplomatic relations at the ambassadorial level.

As testimony to this favorable atmosphere, Nicholas Ridley, appointed by the Conservative administration to the position of minister in charge of the negotiation, traveled to the Malvinas and to Buenos Aires in July 1979, only three months after the new government assumed power. Although Ridley went to the islands to conduct a survey, in his report, Lord Franks confirmed mention of the idea of a leaseback: "Informal soundings of Island Councilors' opinion showed a preference for a lengthy freeze of the dispute and little enthusiasm for the idea of a leaseback" (S. 1, p. 20).

In spite of the Islanders' preferences, upon his return Ridley presented a draft of the negotiating options to Lord Carrington, the new head of the Foreign Office, In it, he leaned toward "substantive negotiations on sovereignty" based on the British and the Islanders' interest in trying to find a solution through negotiation. The Franks Report added: "He suggested that the solution best fitted to meet the government objectives and the wishes of the Islanders would be a leaseback which might be acceptable to the Islanders on the right terms" (Ibid., p. 21).

Ridley's opinion notwithstanding, the administration resolved that at the first bilateral meeting between the Conservatives and the Argentines (which took place in New York in April 1980), it would suggest freezing the sovereignty theme. The suggestion was, of course, rejected by the Argentine delegation.

The Franks Report comments that in June 1980 the Defence Committee revised its position based on the New York meeting and on a new memorandum from Lord Carrington, and then, as Ridley had proposed, "It agreed to attempt to reach a solution on the dispute on the basis of a leaseback arrangement . . . and agreed that Ridley should visit the islands to discover the level of support there for such an arrangement" (Ibid., p. 22).

It was probably at this point, based on the mandate quoted in the Franks Report, that the Foreign Office decided to formulate a "Proposal of Agreement," which I have had access to and which generally consisted of six points. The essence of the proposal was included in the first two points. In the first, title to sovereignty over the Malvinas and its maritime zone was transferred to Argentina as of the date of the agreement. In the second, a leaseback to the United Kingdom was simultaneously effected for a period of 99 years. During those years, a joint administration would be in place to guarantee the Islanders and their descendants the uninterrupted enjoyment of their way of life as well as their British institutions, laws, and customs.

This proposal was never formally presented to the Argentine government, although surely the Argentine ambassador in London knew of its terms and communicated them to the Argentine foreign minister with the confidentiality that the subject required. In any event, in keeping with the goal of this chapter, this is more valid testimony as to the legitimacy of Argentine rights to the Malvinas because, once again, the British government demonstrated its willingness to transfer sovereignty over the islands to Argentina. That transfer was to occur at the end of a long period of time, allowing the Islanders to adjust to the new situation without any trauma, in no way dilutes the implicit recognition of Argentina's title.

Ridley again consults the Islanders on the options for a solution to the dispute. Under the mandate from the Defence Committee, the Foreign Office official responsible for the negotiations traveled to the islands in November 1980. The best source on Ridley's surveys during this visit is the statements of the governor and the Islanders when in early 1983 they were called to testify before the Kershaw Committee. Although their opinions might appear somewhat distorted because of the impact of the armed conflict, they retain the freshness of testimony from those directly involved.

Governor Hunt commented that at the time, Ridley proposed three alternatives: freeze, leaseback, and condominium. Beck confirms this and indicates that Ridley "expressing a preference for a 1,000 year lease but a preparedness to settle for 99 years, discussed this option with the Islanders" (S. 21, p. 120). Ridley even risked naming a time period for the transfer of sovereignty to Argentina—the same one in the agreement with China on Hong Kong.

Hunt added that, among the three alternatives, the Legislative Council overwhelmingly supported a freeze. Asked by Mr. Spearing if there were differences of opinion among the Islanders, he answered: "A minority wanted no conversations with Argentina. There was a minority which was prepared to go to the Argentines and talk about leaseback, but the bulk of the Islanders, as far as I can ascertain, was fully behind the Council" (S. 3, pp. 193–194).

There are different interpretations of the results of this survey, but one of the most credible is that of Mr. Watt, manager of the Malvinas radio station, who conceded that he used this medium to speak to many Kelpers about sovereignty and particularly about the leaseback scheme. Although he admitted that in general people avoided thinking about the options and preferred to believe they did not exist, he added: "Many people liked the idea of leaseback at the time but did not want to come out and say so." Asked if in fact there were many such people, he answered: "Oh indeed yes . . . fifty percent of the population I would say," and on Gran Malvina around 97 percent. (S. 3, pp. 290–292)

Beck, who also mentions Watt's opinion that 50 percent of the Islanders were receptive, adds: "Similarly Sir Nigel Fischer, an MP involved in the United Kingdom Falklands Committee, argued that the leaseback proposals of 1980 offered the last chance of reaching an Anglo-Argentine modus vivendi" (S. 21, p. 121).

To finish this evaluation with an assessment that is less favorable but also less refutable, I quote the Franks Report as it summarizes what Ridley himself reported upon his return from his second visit: "He . . . put forward several possible future policies, including leaseback. On leaseback Islanders' opinion appeared divided, with a substantial minority opposed to it and the majority undecided" (S. 1, p. 23).

In summary, the results of the survey demonstrated a range of opinions that could be termed positive, with a good percentage of those consulted favorable or willing to talk—50 percent and many more on Gran Malvina—and a minority absolutely opposed. We shall soon see that, as generally happens, the militants, whatever their number, ended up having their way.

The hostile reception in Parliament for the secretary of state of the Foreign Office. On December 2, after informing the government of his surveys, Nicholas Ridley appeared before the Lower House of Parliament. Appendix F of the Franks Report (S. 1, pp. 101–105) summarizes the session, the essence of which follows.

Minister Ridley was to be moderate in his presentation: "We have no doubt about our sovereignty over the islands. The Argentines, however, continue to press their claim. The dispute is causing continuing uncertainty, emigration and economic stagnation in the islands." He added that after exploratory conversations with the Argentines in April, the government had considered means for arriving at a solution "which would be acceptable to all parties. In this it is essential that we should be guided by the wishes of the Islanders themselves."

He continued listing the options he had presented, including the freeze and the formula for transfer with a leaseback, and he concluded stating: "The essential elements must be to preserve British administration, the law and the way of life of the Islanders, freeing the maritime resources of the islands blighted by the dispute." And so that there would be no doubt as to the role of the Islanders, he emphasized: "It is for the Islanders to advise on which, if any, option should be explored in negotiations with the Argentines." He asked them to make their point of view known in "due course" and stressed that "any eventual settlement would have to be endorsed by the Islanders."

It would be dishonest to conceal that Parliament's reaction to the minister was hostile, even merciless. His statement was termed disturbing and deeply upsetting, the leaseback scheme shameful. The whole thing amounted to giving up territory for nothing, and the public proposal of transfer with a leaseback was said to have weakened the long-held steadfast position on the subject of sovereignty. In addition to the Islanders' interests, there were other strategic and economic interests to consider.

As to the last point referring to resources, Ridley indicated that this was exactly one of the arguments for seeking a solution acceptable to Argentina. Otherwise, the possibility of declaring a 200-mile fishing zone was remote, to which was added investors' fear of the threat—he used the expression "dead hand"—of the dispute with Argentina. Regarding respect for the Kelpers' opinions, Minister Ridley was categorical:

The details of any leaseback arrangement would first have to be considered by the Islanders and then it would be subject to negotiations . . . with the Argentine, and then the subject of endorsement by the Islanders and this House. (S. 1, p. 105)

However, he refused to affirm that if the Islanders point of view were favorable to the status quo, he would accept it, saying that such anticipation was somewhat hypothetical.

The session ended with a request to postpone, as one representative alleged, "because of the intense dissatisfaction I feel about what the Minister said."

This debate should be noted because it is highly instructive. Although the minister's presentation included a double consultation with the Kelpers (including something of a veto power through the endorsement of what the parties agreed to), and the possibility of a second veto lay in submitting to Parliament for approval the agreements that had been reached, Ridley was abused by his colleagues in Parliament. Surely much of this hostile reaction to Ridley's proposal was due to the fact that after five years of military government, there were no valid spokespersons of the Argentine people before the representatives of the British people.

Nonetheless, I have a minor criticism of Ridley's presentation. I think that he should have omitted his initial statement about having no doubt regarding British title to the islands. After my analysis in the first chapter, I find it difficult to believe he really believed that. He based his statement on a linear argument almost exclusively structured around economic interests tied to natural resources, alienating the theoreticians—who fortunately are always there—and those who considered their own economic interests better safeguarded by the status quo.

Furthermore, in addition to this hostile treatment in Parliament, the media joined in the criticism of the government in a campaign unquestionably orchestrated by the groups with vested interests in the islands. In this connection, Beck says:

> The *Times* reinforced the parliamentary campaign . . . and both reactions effectively killed the policy initiative in spite of the British government's perception that there was no alternative to the leaseback idea which stood any chance of solving the dispute. (Ibid., p. 121)

Because of misinformation, because of chauvinism, and because of arrogance, the way of reason was closed and the way of passion opened. Because of the economic and also political interests of a small group of individuals—in Port Stanley and in London—on December 2, 1980, without anyone's being aware of it, the prologue was being written to a drama into which the two peoples would be dragged 15 months later.

The British goal: Negotiate to buy time and win the Islanders over to this proposal. After that day in the British Parliament, events occurred in rapid succession. The following chronology is from the Franks Report.

January 6, 1981: The Islanders, encouraged by their success, anticipated events and requested that the British government "should seek an agreement to freeze the dispute over sovereignty for a special period of time" (S. 1, p. 23).

January 29, 1981: The Defence Committee determined that although unacceptable, there was a mandate from the islands to negotiate and stated its opinion that "the aim should be to keep negotiations going" and, while applying no pressure, to let the Islanders see the need to explore a realistic settlement based on leaseback (Ibid.).

February 1981: The second round of negotiations took place in New York; two Islanders were among the British delegation. The United Kingdom proposed a freeze, which was flatly rejected by the Argentine side (Ibid., p. 24). One account suggests that Ridley conversed informally with the head of the Argentine delegation about the leaseback proposal referred to above, although we know of no official record of this.

May 1981: In Buenos Aires, Ambassador Anthony Williams urgently called for a new round of negotiations (which would include the issue of sovereignty) before the end of the year in order to avoid serious deterioration of relations with Argentina (Ibid.).

An extensive meeting took place to review island policy, in which John Ure, assistant undersecretary for Latin America of the Foreign Office—who had just visited Argentina and the Malvinas—presented a memorandum. In it he said he was under the impression that in the islands "opinion had not hardened irrevocably against leaseback . . . but much more would need to be done to educate Islanders and United Kingdom opinion about the danger of inaction." He suggested a number of measures: assurances to the Islanders on access to the United Kingdom; a resettlement scheme for those dissatisfied; further land distribution; and the initiation of more productive economic schemes for the islands. (Ibid., p. 25) Ure evaluated a solution with transfer of sovereignty to Argentina and so wanted guarantees provided to Kelpers who might want to emigrate.

June 10, 1981: Anthony Williams sent a lengthy cable saying that ground had been lost since February, that Argentina had less patience, and that the Islanders were increasingly further from reality. He added that if the only practicable solution were some form of negotiated leaseback, it was clear that it would not be acceptable without "some kind of sales campaign . . . bringing home to British opinion the potential cost of any alternative." If the government did not undertake one, Argentina might conclude that the United Kingdom was "only bamboozling without any basic intention of reaching a mutually acceptable settlement." (Ibid., p. 26) A clear message from a British professional.

July 20, 1981: Ridley sent a draft to Lord Carrington in which he mentioned that elections in the islands would result in a new Legislative Council "opposed to substantive talks on sovereignty with Argentina." He also stated that Argentine patience "would then run out" and by early 1982 retaliatory action must be expected: in the first instance through the withdrawal of communications, fuel, and other facilities it provided; and in the long run, in "some form of military action." He then examined the options open, mentioning as the first "to open negotiations on leaseback with or without Islanders' concurrence or participation but with the result subject to the Islanders' and parliamentary approval—then to embark on a "public education campaign or to let Argentina conclude that the government would not discuss sovereignty." (Ibid., p. 27) He declared himself in favor of the education campaign. An exceptional picture of the situation from the head of the bilateral negotiations.

July 27, 1981: Argentine Foreign Minister Oscar Camilión delivered a note to Ambassador Williams expressing the Argentine government's serious concern about the lack of progress in New York and stressing that the next round of negotiations could not be merely an exploratory exercise but should mark the beginning "of a decisive stage towards the definitive termination of the dispute." Simultaneously, the Argentine Foreign Ministry issued a press communiqué reporting this note and saying that "the acceleration of negotiations on the Malvinas, with resolution and with clear objectives in view had become an unpostponable priority for its foreign policy." (Ibid., p. 28)

Within eight months, bilateral deterioration was glaring and it was clearly the fault of the United Kingdom. Something resembling collective political cowardice led them to recognize at all levels that leaseback was the only realistic solution and at the same time to put it aside.

In fact, at the end of July, Minister Ridley, who was directly responsible for negotiations with Argentina, without deciding against the scheme mentioned, postponed it until a public campaign paved the way for its eventual acceptance. That meant that whereas Argentina, fed up with the runaround of 15 years of discussions, firmly demanded an acceleration of the rhythm of the negotiations, no one on the British side wanted to exert the necessary political authority to point this exercise seriously toward a solution acceptable to both parties. The British instead proposed an educational campaign, and I assume a persuasive one, that by nature was incompatible with the timing required by the Argentine side.

But things did not stop there because the British admitted that Lord Carrington "did not accept this course of action"—according to what he might have told Lord Franks—because in his opinion "such a campaign would not have been agreed to by his colleagues and would have been counterproductive" (S. 1, p. 28). It was only a dramatic demonstration "that the political price of compromise would be higher than the governments of both main parties were willing to pay" (S. 29, p. 40).

The beginning of the end: The United Kingdom is left without a negotiating position. If the head of the Foreign Office did not accept the proposal of his minister, Nicholas Ridley, to initiate a persuasion campaign—directed at the Islanders and at London political circles—one wonders what the United Kingdom was willing to put on the negotiating table. The response is blunt but simple: absolutely nothing.

I must point out that everything I have written on the alternatives the British government was cooking up comes from the report in which Margaret Thatcher commissioned Lord Franks to define political responsibility in the armed conflict. For sale to the public at a price of 6.10 pounds, the report constitutes a public confession of the grandeur and misery of that period. In many cases it is based on official documents, previously classified secret, that British parliamentarian democracy has sought to reveal, a gesture that I acknowledge and applaud. This occurred, for example, with a document dated September 14, 1981, sent by Lord Carrington to the prime minister, on the options in the Malvinas question, which I shall enumerate.

In an abstract, the head of the Foreign Office—who was about to meet with Foreign Minister Camilión in New York—refers to the Argentine note and communiqué mentioned above (which had been circulated in the United Nations) and expresses his conviction

   i. "that leaseback still provided the most likely, and perhaps the only basis for an agreed solution of the dispute";

  ii. that the position of the Islanders in this respect was not favorable and that "there was little prospect of doing more than keeping some sort of negotiations with Argentina going";

 iii. that this could lead to some retaliatory measures and the risk of "a military confrontation with Argentina could not be discounted"; and

 iv. that contingency studies that included supplying and defending the islands "would be both difficult and costly." (S. 1, p. 29)

I reiterate: nothing! Because in i. and ii. he suggests continuing some kind of negotiation—but he does not say on what! All that is left standing is, on one hand, the warning about risks and, on the other, the final option, which had always been discarded as the most negative: "Fortress Falklands," in spite of its difficulty and cost.

At the time, in September 1981, there was an interesting exchange of correspondence between the director of the Latin America department of the Foreign Office and the British ambassador in Buenos Aires. In his letter, the former, Mr. Fearn, admits: "The domestic political constraints must at this stage continue to prevent us from taking any steps which might be interpreted as putting pressure on the Islanders or overruling their wishes" (S. 1, p. 28). Ambassador Williams answers, terming the British attitude "Micawberism"—for Dickens's accommodating character—and pinpointing the lack of a negotiating strategy. "The unguided wishes of the Falkland Islanders," he notes, "were very, very unlikely . . . to provide even a grudging form of acceptance of sovereignty transfer in any form. . . . It would be better to tell the Argentines frankly and face the consequences" (Ibid., p. 30). As a former Foreign Office official said, "Making bricks without straw became an essential skill for Britain's diplomats" (S. 29, p. 26).

But the governor of the Malvinas was not dissuaded as to sovereignty, and on January 19, 1982—three months before the occupation of the islands by Argentina—he submitted his annual report for 1981. In it he points out that relations between the Islanders and Argentina had deteriorated during the year and that "Islanders had hardened against leaseback. In consequence the Governor saw no way ahead in future talks" (Ibid., p. 35). In the Foreign Office's detailed evaluation of Hunt's report, Mr. Fearn observed that during 1981 "the leaseback initiative had run into the ground and the Islanders had moved to open support of the Fortress Falklands policy. Leaseback was now 'effectively dead'" (Ibid., p. 35). And it concludes that there remains no other alternative but to drift toward an open confrontation (Ibid.).

Because I consider it of such interest, I have detailed the British version of the factors that killed what the British themselves had termed the last serious and realistic proposal for a solution to the sovereignty dispute between the two countries.

Part of the goal of this chapter is that each reader deduce whether indeed any political will to formally set forth this proposal existed in the Foreign Office and at the various levels of the Conservative administration. This would have implied, nothing more and nothing less, than the transfer of the Malvinas Islands to Argentine sovereignty. In the context of Argentine rights, it is unimportant whether this happens after a term of years—be it 50, 70, or 99—which represents nothing in the life of a nation.

Although it goes beyond the scope of this chapter, the preceding analysis has revealed absolute responsibility on the part of the British in that the scheme has not become a reality. In addition to more glaring reasons—the militancy of the Islanders' interests and cowardice in confronting a domestic political erosion—it is appropriate to indicate the low priority the British cabinet traditionally assigned to the Malvinas question—until the events of 1982 catapulted it to the front page of every newspaper in the world.

A COMPREHENSIVE EVALUATION OF THE BRITISH PROPOSALS AND THEIR FUTURE APPLICATION

For final analysis of each of the proposals set forth by the British over 15 years of bilateral negotiations, there could be no more appropriate colophon than the reflections by the Committee of Representatives of the British people, which considered the proposals in a comprehensive form.

In truth, the report conducted by Lord Kershaw could not omit commenting on the essence of the proposals that I have analyzed throughout this chapter. I believe the evaluation of the Foreign Affairs Committee of the House of Commons to be of marked importance, all the more so because the latter will be called upon to register its opinion of any agreement reached on the future of the Malvinas.

This document attributes decisive implications to the first proposal analyzed and says that the offer of transfer of sovereignty in the Memorandum of Understanding "colored all subsequent discussions between the two governments and provided fertile soil in which Argentina's subsequent sense of grievance and betrayal could grow" (S. 6, p. xviii). It states:

> In subsequent negotiations the United Kingdom saw itself constrained on one hand by its original concession on the possibility of transfer of sovereignty and on the other by the hardening of the attitude of the elected representatives of the islands against that possibility. (S. 4, p. xxix)

The first draft report recognizes that the Islands Council "may not have fully reflected the views of the Falkland population as a whole" (Ibid.). Insinuating that they had been manipulated by a small nucleus, it adds—in both the draft report and the approved version—in order not to be accused of bad faith, they were compelled to negotiate "but to enter into negotiations on each occasion with their hands tied" (S. 6, p. xix).

I must confess that I am a little confused by the business of good and bad faith. In my opinion, in the latter case, one appears to negotiate when in reality "one's hands are tied" throughout, instead of seeking enough political leeway to do it with honesty. But perhaps this is a flaw in my perception, or a problem caused by geographic latitudes or cultural patterns, as we have seen in other fields.

The Kershaw Report continues quoting without great detail all of this important negotiating process regarding which, naturally, it does not want to explore in great depth:

> In this process several compromise proposals were tried out by the British government on both the Argentine government and the Falklands Legislative Council. . . . The most important of these were the possibility of a shared administration (or condominium) and the possibility of a leaseback agreement, under which both Argentine sovereignty and British administration could simultaneously be recognised. (S. 6, p. xix)

Unfortunately, the definitive version of the Kershaw Report omitted several paragraphs containing opinions that, because they came from such a qualified source, acquired special significance in the study of this stage of the negotiations. Naturally, they might have eventually appeared somewhat compromising. One of them stated: "It was, perhaps, unfortunate that the British government failed accurately to assess the islanders' opinion before conceding the single most important point at issue between the two countries" (S. 4, p. xxix).

This is interesting because it confirms that in 1968 the position was to concede sovereignty to Argentina, but I do not share the point of view that gave rise to it. What in my opinion is unfortunate is that successive British administrations have allowed a small group of individuals subjected to an anachronistic "colonial situation" to dictate to the government of the United Kingdom the conduct to be followed in an international dispute, the gravity of which was demonstrated in the events of 1982.

What appears unacceptable to me is that the first draft of the Kershaw report recognizes what is inferred from a reading of the Franks Report. It says that the latter document makes evident that the government of the United Kingdom "although ostensibly an independent party in the negotiations was increasingly forced to play the role of honest broker between Argentina and the Falklands" (S. 4, p. xxix).

William Wallace, who gave his article the provocative title "How Frank Was Franks?," says, "If at the end of March 1982 there was, for both Argentina and Britain, no apparent alternative to confrontation, it was because diplomacy had failed largely because of the contradictory signals given over the previous two years by the British government" (S. 12, p. 454).

I am convinced that these last appraisals from British sources exempt me from further commentary. Analyzing each one of the proposals by the United Kingdom, I have reflected on what each represents as an acknowledgment of the legitimacy of Argentina's rights to the southern archipelagoes. These last assessments by such a distinguished British forum not only confirm the conclusion concerning Argentina's rights but also bring out the moral responsibility that those who preferred to ignore them must assume for the dramatic events unleashed soon thereafter.

We are left to conclude that these ideas, initiatives, and even concrete proposals have not lost currency, although they are logically encapsulated by the impasse in which the 1982 conflict in the South Atlantic placed the negotiations over the sovereignty dispute. In the next chapters I will again take up evaluations of them, because as the Kershaw Report concludes on the leaseback: "The passage of time may well make possible a reopening of discussions along these lines" (S. 6, p. lxiii).

3

The Third British Dilemma:
The Necessity of Involving
Argentina in the Institutional Future
of the Southern Archipelagoes

===

AN INESCAPABLE CHALLENGE

When several members of the Kershaw Committee traveled to the Malvinas in January 1983 to hear the views of the Islanders, the following dialogue took place:

> *Mr. Canavan:* Does it mean you think that the option of status quo, a "British Colony" and "Fortress Falklands," is untenable?
>
> *Mrs. Davidson:* I cannot see the British government allowing it to continue indefinitely. I do not myself want to be responsible for another conflict and 250 more lives lost in the South Atlantic, so therefore we should face up to the fact that we cannot remain like this.
>
> *Mr. Canavan:* You are saying that some constitutional change is necessary to ensure greater stability to these islands and more security for the people within them?
>
> *Mrs. Davidson:* Yes I do. I think we should also face up to the fact that it will involve Argentina. (S. 3, p. 239)

This dialogue, which took place when the aftermath of the conflict was still fresh in the Kelpers' minds, concludes with a kernel of common sense. Really, the United Kingdom is currently confronting a third challenge: how to incorporate Argentina into the institutional framework that will resolve the dispute over the southern archipelagoes, and how to do so in such a way as to ensure political stability and economic prosperity in the region.

The report drafted by the Foreign Affairs Committee of the House of Commons shares this point of view and, after referring to theoretical unilateral British options, concludes:

> Neither solution, however, is likely to be acceptable to Argentina, and therefore neither would achieve the objective of resolving the dispute or of dispensing with the need for a substantial continued British military presence in the islands. In the long run a solution acceptable to the Falklands' immediate neighbors is essential to the Islanders themselves; neither independence nor incorporation to the United Kingdom could conceivably achieve that objective. (S. 6, pp. xxii, lxiv)

The preceding paragraphs are only a preview of what follows. I dedicate this third chapter—relying as usual on British sources—to documenting the United Kingdom's clear understanding of the need to consider Argentina's interests. This assessment takes on vital importance given that what has to be negotiated in a timely fashion is not whether it is appropriate to involve Argentina, but how to do it. That is, which of the possible alternatives is acceptable and best responds to the interests of all parties concerned? In Chapter 4, I analyze exactly which parameters must be taken into account at the time of substantive negotiations.

FORTRESS FALKLANDS

An option that had been discarded until the 1982 conflict.

After questioning one of the Islanders, a Kershaw Committee member who traveled to the islands, Mr. Townsend, stated, "It became clear from the Franks Report that Lord Carrington thought Fortress Falklands would be the worst of the three options" (S. 3, p. 216).

In reality, the alternative of fortifying the Malvinas had always been excluded by successive British administrations, even in the context of crises such as the one that arose in 1975 due to the failure of the British to respond to Argentina's repeated claims.

There is abundant proof of Mr. Townsend's assertion. In May 1979, in October of the same year, and in July 1981, Fortress Falklands was among the alternatives on the Malvinas question that Nicholas Ridley, the official responsible for the negotiations with Argentina, or Lord Carrington, the head of the Foreign Office, presented to the prime minister. And in every case it was ruled out as the least appropriate. The remaining options included the possibility of abandoning the islands (and relocating the Islanders), bilateral talks without any concessions on the subject of sovereignty, and substantial negotiations with Argentina. The latter option was chosen as the course of action to be pursued.

Peter Beck also approaches this subject and relates its treatment by the Defence Committee in July 1980 saying:

> Guided by FCO studies and an appreciation of Argentine pressure for "a more dynamic pace of progress" it reviewed future strategies. The "Fortress Falklands" option, involving the termination of negotiations, the risk of an Argentine invasion, and the difficulty of either defending or recapturing the islands was ruled out as impracticable. (S. 21, p. 120)

There is no doubt then that until the 1982 conflict, the plan to establish a military base in the islands, the so-called Fortress Falklands, was basically a theoretical option within the cabinet. It was part of the classic technical exercise, common to all foreign ministries, of offering alternatives for consideration. It had never been seriously analyzed, and when it was, in the context of deteriorating bilateral relations, it was ruled out as impracticable, in spite of the pressure to the contrary by Island interest groups.

After the conflict:
Fortress Falklands, a politico-military reality.

When the armed conflict ended on June 14 with the Argentine surrender, the British government decided to restructure the defense of the islands by building a powerful military complex in the Malvinas. The Fortress Falklands option became a fact incorporated into the changing history of the archipelago. Walter Little, professor of political science and Latin American studies at the University of Liverpool, describes this new attitude:

> Prior to the war this had consisted of a handful of marines. Clearly this had failed and it was generally agreed that any future defensive capability must be substantive and not merely symbolic. The new arrangements involved the construction of an airfield capable of taking long-haul aircraft so as to allow rapid reinforcement in time of need, an early-warning detection and interception capability, ground-to-air missile defences, and enough rapid-response capability to be able to deter certain minor landings. (S. 14, p. 152)

Little, whose information dates through 1988, addresses the problem of costs on the basis of a statement in Parliament justifying the reconstruction for defense purposes. In this connection he says:

> In the period of 1982–87 some 3,010 million pounds have been spent and the official estimate of annual garrisoning costs from 1988 onwards amounts to around 100 million pounds a year. When compared with expenditure in 1984–85 of nearly 700 million pounds, the case would seem to have been made for some savings. However there are a number of

aspects—such as the diversion of troops, support costs, maintenance of sophisticated equipment, etc.—which need to be stressed more than they have been. (Ibid., p. 153)

Little likewise explains that commitments in the South Atlantic have imposed a considerable burden on the United Kingdom's responsibilities within NATO: "Two years after the completion of the airfield some three thousand troops are still deployed at a probable real cost of several hundred million pounds a year." He says that the army is far from happy about what they privately regard "as the diversion from Britain's real priorities (the navy is less discontented with out-of-area commitments), but their reservations are not likely to bring about major changes." (Ibid., p. 154)

Although it may be true that costs have decreased and stabilized during recent years, the considerations set forth to the Islanders by Mr. Hooley, a member of the Kershaw Commission, are still valid: "But is it feasible for 1,800 people here to see themselves as British and to determine foreign policy and indeed defence policy, involving millions of pounds in public expenditure, over fifty million people in the United Kingdom?" And he also asked, "Is it fair? Is it democratic?" And he concluded, "Do you think it rather strange that there is no other similar group of people in the United Kingdom with that degree of paramountcy?" (S. 3, p. 274)

Peter Beck believes that substantial political, fiscal, and economic post-1982 commitments—such as the large (albeit decreasing) garrison presence and the Mount Pleasant airfield—demonstrate that in spite of the rhetoric and the impression of Fortress Falklands as a fantasy, "the British government has become locked into this type of policy, at least in the short-term. The policy of long-term realism is a matter for debate" (S. 21, p. 143)

As to the long term, and also the medium term, it should be mentioned that the Kelpers' customs have been seriously affected by Fortress Falklands to the point where a Kelper, a Mr. King, admitted that they were very worried and, compared to the Argentine presence during the conflict, they preferred the British presence because "we have to take the lesser of the two evils" (S. 3, p. 216). This lesser, but still somewhat detestable evil, had become more serious with time, and newspaper articles relate other problems in the relationships between very different groups of human beings who share daily life in the Malvinas. This means that the military presence has changed the Islanders' lifestyle, respect for which was always considered of paramount interest by successive British governments.

We have here a series of commentaries that suggest the necessity of reflecting on the rationality of an option chosen under extreme circumstances. In this connection, Beck's commentaries, which he terms evaluations, on Fortress Falklands are highly valid:

a. The basic sovereignty problem remains unresolved; indeed, there exists the risk of further conflict.

b. The policy imposes substantial cost (defence, diplomatic and economic). It has been regarded variously as a "costly anachronism and an appalling diversion of resources."

c. The policy raises questions about the relevance of a South Atlantic role for a NATO/European power while recently Vice Admiral Sir J. Woodward conceded that the Falkland Islands are not a very good area for military training in the NATO complex.

d. Before 1982, British governments without exception rejected the alternative of "Fortress Falklands."

e. The policy offers short-term security but long-term uncertainty in the context of changing political, military and fiscal circumstances. (S. 21, p. 143)

In the most blunt and concise pronouncement on the subject to date, the Committee on Latin American Affairs of the Liberal Party said that a change in British policy is imperative, because Fortress Falklands was "political madness" (S. 30, p. 2). And let us not forget that a politician of the stature of Edward Heath alluded to the uncertainty regarding security, and he did so after the conflict.

With all the doubts and difficulties now raised, what is sure is that, as Mr. Hooley pointed out, although for the time being it might be inevitable, this "does not remove the fact that we have to look beyond the 'Fortress Falkland' situation" (S. 3, p. 256).

This is, in fact, an imperative, if what is wanted is to ensure stability and political security for the area and to optimize the exploitation of its natural resources. In Chapter 5 another possible option will be discussed, which might eventually bring about a solution to this case.

ANGLO-ARGENTINE UNDERSTANDING AS A REQUISITE FOR THE EXPLOITATION OF NATURAL RESOURCES

A description of the scenario:
The economic potential of the archipelagoes in dispute.

The economic potential to which I refer is not on the islands themselves; rather, the Malvinas, like South Georgia and South Sandwich, have, according to international law, maritime zones belonging to the coastal state. It is well known that these jurisdictions have acquired great significance over time. Today, according to the regime adopted in 1983 at the Law of the Sea Conference after arduous and prolonged negotiations lasting more than a decade, it is commonly recognized that they include 12 miles of territorial sea, an Exclusive Economic Zone (EEZ) extending another 188 miles, and the continental shelf extending to its outer limit.

With regard to the southern archipelagoes involved in the sovereignty dispute, these criteria apply to a very extensive jurisdictional area with a considerable real and potential economic value.

Beck, alluding to Lord Shackleton's 1976 report, notes that in spite of showing the Falkland Islands as a territory caught in a process of demographic, economic, and social decline, a number of potential growth areas were identified, including "offshore resources such as fish, krill, oil and alginates. The 'enormous potential' of fishing, most notable of krill, was adjudged capable of underpinning the Islands' future economic viability" (S. 21, p. 113). Beck adds that

> the aftermath of the 1973 oil crisis, in association with North Sea oil developments and the geological surveys conducted in the Falklands region (especially the one undertaken during 1973–75 by Professor Griffiths of the Birmingham University for the Foreign Office), gave added interest to the prospects for offshore oil and natural gas. (Ibid., p. 113)

On this matter of the real extent of the natural resources of the archipelagoes involved in the controversy, I must quote the relevant part of a Foreign Office memorandum—to which the departments of commerce and defense contributed—that refers to its potential, time periods for exploitation, and means:

> *Hydrocarbons:* The available data do not permit an assessment of whether hydrocarbons exist in waters around the Falkland Islands and the Dependencies. More detailed seismic surveys and, if the findings justify it, exploratory drilling would be necessary before any judgment could be made. It is very unlikely that hydrocarbons exist on the islands themselves. There is even less knowledge of the prospects in the areas of South Georgia and South Sandwich Islands, where the waters' depths and weather conditions make explorations more difficult.
>
> *Minerals:* There is no evidence.
>
> *Fish:* The potential of the waters around the Falklands and Dependencies is considerable. The British fishing industry has, however, shown no interest in such distant waters. (S. 4, p. 6)

The reference to living resources is laconic, but really the term "considerable" is very modest, because the potential in the area is such that it has already attracted major fishing fleets—Japanese, Polish, Spanish, Soviet, East German, and in recent years Taiwanese and South Korean—in the 200-mile area (EEZ) off the Malvinas and the South Georgia Islands.

The Anglo-Argentine dispute and lack of any agreement in 15 years of negotiations have turned one of the richest fishing zones into a maritime area free of any regulation; that is, it has become the high seas. Even after the 1982 conflict, the Protection Zone declared by the United Kingdom applied only to Argentine vessels, and fishing activity rapidly intensified. In 1984, there were 250 active vessels and in 1986 there were 600.

This implies a high risk of predatory practices, as the FAO has recognized since 1983, indicating the growing need for cooperation to ensure the rational use of fishing resources.

Regarding the resources of the continental shelf—oil, gas, and minerals such as manganese nodules and others—I believe that the information stated by the British Foreign Ministry is a bit ambiguous. I have turned to another memorandum on the presence of hydrocarbons, drafted, at the request of the Kershaw Commission, by Professor Griffiths, mentioned above, and Peter Baker. This document, after noting the five stages that are technically recognized as part of the evaluation regarding the existence of hydrocarbons, provides specifics for both the Falkland Islands region and the Dependencies.

Falkland Islands region. Knowledge of the area around the Falkland Islands is at present stuck within Stage 3 (industry financial involvement precedes Stage 4, drilling, and Stage 5, production) and the reason given is of interest: "because of political uncertainties." And it continues:

> We were involved in a marine geophysical reconnaissance (Stage 2) of the region 1973–75 on behalf of the FCO. Since then three separate detailed speculative surveys have been undertaken by prospecting companies and sold nonexclusively to several oil companies. (S. 4, p. 100)

The memorandum I am quoting coincides with that of the Foreign Office in that all the drilling is offshore. It mentions the Malvinas Basin—to the west and southwest of the islands—the closest and similar to the Magellan Basin, and the Falklands Plateau—to the east—stating that only the first arouses any interest on the part of industry. "In the longer term (ten to twenty years) however, as extraction technology develops, this very large area should also become of interest, since the geology is favorable to hydrocarbons accumulation." And the same document adds:

> Burdwood Bank, south of the Falkland islands, has also received the attention of the industry. We would not rate it so highly as a hydrocarbons prospect, however, because more recent tectonic disturbances will have disrupted the older sediments, easing the escape of previously trapped oil and gas . . . but it might be of interest in small highly biogenetic basins. (S. 4, p. 101)

In summary—an assessment shared by Argentine technicians—the majority of deposits of greatest potential value (the Malvinas Basin or Burdwood Bank) are in areas of the continental shelf, which even the

British recognize as belonging to Argentina. Of similar interest are the western and southwestern sectors of Gran Malvina's shelf, which geologically is nothing more than a prolongation of the Argentine coastline.

As for South Georgia and South Sandwich archipelagoes, the memorandum notes the following:

Falkland Island Dependencies. The only real prospect within this area is the Falkland Plateau (to the East of the archipelago), already mentioned. . . . What is said above of the Burdwood Bank, including South Georgia, nothing we have seen to date (Stage 1, reconnaissance) gives any indication of the likelihood of hydrocarbons accumulations, but the possibility cannot be ruled out entirely. The same is true also of the South Sandwich Islands region. (Ibid.)

Asked in the same forum to expand upon his memorandum, Professor Griffiths considered speculative all estimates on the volume of oil and gas in the area. He believed that the costs "will be many times more expensive (than the North Sea) and the technology has not yet been developed to do it but it will not take many years to develop it." And he risked a global assessment:

So I think that probably companies will be interested in having a look [in the Falkland Islands] within the next ten years because they are always looking many years ahead of exploiting, but I would not think that they would be exploiting within perhaps twenty. (S. 4, p. 107)

If these time-scale estimates are correct, and if one considers that by 1991 eight of the ten years had gone by, the conclusion is that by arriving at a satisfactory political agreement, the most advanced stages of prospecting necessary to seriously evaluate the potential of the area—specifically drilling—should begin relatively soon. Obviously, actual exploitation will depend on the economic interest the deposits arouse in the industry.

In the last chapter we shall see that, at the end of 1991, preliminary contacts finally began, among them the effort to stake out maritime jurisdictions, an event that assumes political agreement at the highest level. To initiate any activity in the evaluation of the deposits, agreement is necessary.

Taking into account the limited information available in some cases, we now have something of an idea of the importance of the natural resources involved. Let us then see how they affect our subject.

*Natural resources in the context
of the sovereignty dispute.*

As we have seen, the need to control the indiscriminate harvest of living resources, and the growing interest in exploiting both this fishing wealth and nonrenewable resources, has motivated the British since the mid-1970s to channel initiatives toward negotiating joint administrative arrangements with Argentina.

Peter Beck, who has perhaps among all the writers consulted most carefully followed this question, recalls that

> early in 1977 Anthony Crosland, the British Foreign Minister, warned Parliament . . . we cannot let this situation drag on. . . . [The islands] face an uncertain economic future. The economy is stagnant. . . . It is cooperation and not confrontation . . . which we seek to achieve. (S. 21, p. 115)

And he states that this arrangement was followed by Crosland's successors, Owen and Ridley. He concludes with a sentence with which I totally agree: "In this manner, both Labour and Conservative governments contrasted the positive politico-economic benefits of a framework for Anglo-Argentine economic cooperation with the alleged cost of preserving the status quo" (Ibid.).

Beck notes the assessments of the Shackleton report of May 1976 to the effect that "a more stable and effective Anglo-Argentine relationship constituted an essential prerequisite for an acceptable present for the Islanders," and concludes that the political implications appear inseparable from the economic. He adds: "It is logical therefore that in any major new developments of the Islands' economy, especially those relating to the exploitation of offshore resources, cooperation with Argentina—even participation—should, if possible, be secured" (Ibid., pp. 113–114).

This political approach coincides with the traditional approach of the British business sector. Coalite, Ltd., a holding company that acquired the all-powerful Falkland Islands Company, indicated in its annual report of 1978–1979 that "the removal of uncertainties over external claims regarding sovereignty would greatly help its prospects in the islands" (Ibid., p. 115).

Beck mentions as an example the project to extract alginate from the algae so plentiful in the Malvinas. Investments were suspended in 1976 given the political uncertainty.

The British agreed that Argentine participation was appropriate in an adequate exploitation of natural resources, which should be considered indispensable when the time of nonrenewable resources comes.

The Argentine posture, particularly up to the time of the South Atlantic conflict, has been cautious. According to the principles underlying its position, Argentina cannot grant the United Kingdom jurisdiction over areas belonging to the coastal state, because to do so would legitimize usurpation. Only in negotiations with the Labour administration in 1978, in which both parties had reserved their relative positions, could this precaution be set aside.

The global evaluation completed, the next section will outline the latest events regarding natural resources, which clearly take on particular importance.

The United Kingdom declares a Fishing
Conservation Zone around the Malvinas.

On October 29, 1986, the British government in a "Declaration on Southwest Atlantic Fisheries" claimed the entitlement of the Falkland Islands, based on international law, to a fishing zone around the islands extending the maximum 200 nautical miles. It likewise anticipated that the government of the islands would adopt conservation and administration measures. On the same day, the governor of the islands, Gordon Wesley Jewkes, read a proclamation creating a Falkland Islands Interim Conservation and Management Zone (FICZ) extending over a 150-mile radius from a central point located in the San Carlos Channel, which separates the two principal islands in the Malvinas archipelago. It should be emphasized that the measure did not include the South Georgias or the South Sandwich Islands.

Until the armed conflict of 1982, the United Kingdom had claimed only the territorial sea around the Malvinas Islands, with a traditional jurisdiction of just 3 miles. Successive British governments had always hesitated to extend that area, and when the 200-mile EEZ was declared, it took into account the Argentine position of not recognizing Britain's right to do so. Without accepting this position as correct, they were conscious that they were committing an unfriendly act.

This manner of proceeding with caution lasted even after the armed conflict of 1982, as can be inferred from the vagueness of the first draft report of the Kershaw Committee. Even more, these serious doubts persisted in London in spite of pressure from the Islanders' lobby and an express request from the Legislative Council of the Malvinas with the object of controlling unlimited fishing and providing for income, through licensing, that would permit a balancing of the Islands' budget. Testimony to this is the opinion expressed in the final report adopted by the Committee of the House of Commons to the effect that the measure was inappropriate: "Despite the environmental drawbacks of the existing free-for-all in Falkland waters, we are not convinced that the establishment of an EEZ in Falkland waters can be justified" (S. 6, p. lii, paragraph 145). And it clarifies:

> There is undoubtedly a strong case for the regulation and licensing of fishing in the area of the Falklands and Dependencies, but there are considerable political and practical problems to be overcome. In the first place, if it were not for the existence of the sovereignty dispute, it is a

matter which would be expected to be pursued in consultation with the Falklands neighbors, including Argentina. In the second place, there must be doubts about the international acceptability of a unilaterally-imposed zone particularly amongst third-world and communist countries. In consequence, the policing of such a zone would raise difficult legal problems and would be likely to be expensive . . . which would increase rather than reduce, the need for a large naval presence in the South Atlantic. (S. 6, p. lii, paragraph 146)

In the relevant part of the "Main Conclusions and Recommendations," the Kershaw Committee took its position without resorting to euphemisms:

Although there is undoubtedly a strong case for the regulation and licensing of fishing in the area of the Falklands and Dependencies we are not convinced that the establishment of an Exclusive fishing zone can be justified, in view of the considerable political and practical problems to be overcome. (Ibid., p. lxiv, section xxvi)

In the same year, 1983, even Lady Young, the secretary of state, while testifying before the committee, acknowledged that, although Lord Shackleton had recognized the declaration of 200 miles as appropriate, "it is rather more complicated than other 200-mile fishing zones for other countries and that is why it is still being considered by the government" (S. 6, p. 138).

Why then did the Thatcher administration adopt such a complicated measure that was also legally questionable and politically offensive? Peter Beck tells the story of this decision based on fishing agreements that Argentina signed with the Soviet Union and Bulgaria on July 28 and 29, 1986, respectively, which permitted fishing vessels from those countries access to Argentine territorial waters measured from the coast of Patagonia. In these agreements, the area is defined somewhat imprecisely, and in certain parts, currently in the region to the southwest of the Malvinas, the EEZ that is indisputably Argentina's overlaps with the 200 miles claimed by the Malvinas. The United Kingdom took advantage of the situation and adopted its decision. It was a measure that had been "filed away" for almost a decade and that the United Kingdom obviously applied after feeling increasing pressure.

Rejected as politically expedient by Argentina, this point of view suggests that, in addition to the provocation of these accords, the River Plate country "exhausted the multilateral scheme" based on initiatives in New York with the United States acting as a mediator and with some intervention by the FAO, encouraged by the United Kingdom. Beck says then: "Britain noting Argentine bilateralism and the delay of the multilateral scheme, decides on unilateral action to secure orderly fishing" (S. 21, p. 186).

It is certain that Argentina did not favor—nor does it now favor—an arrangement that multilateralizes responsibility for the conservation of the fishing wealth of the area. This approach includes recognition of the United Kingdom as a coastal state in the area, which is totally unacceptable for Argentina because it contradicts its well-known position. However, it has not opposed technical studies undertaken by the FAO.

Clearly, Palacio San Martín—the seat of the Argentine Foreign Ministry—believes that controlling the harvest, which is absolutely necessary, was and is the responsibility of the parties involved in the sovereignty dispute. The most effective and appropriate solution lies in reaching an understanding on the basic conflict, to which the fishing issue is intimately connected.

It should be noted that the 1986 British decision has not prevented the persistence of political and practical problems, as the members of the Foreign Affairs Committee of the House of Commons warn. With respect to political problems, the British measure drew a vigorous protest from the Argentine government, which sought and obtained wide international support against it. Peter Beck refers to this serious event in his latest work:

> Argentina challenged the "illegal" British action, a view supported by the Argentina-Brazilian-Uruguayan-Punta del Este meeting (2 November 1986), by the OAS (November 1986) and by the Non-Aligned Movement (March 1987). In February 1987 the Inter-American Legal Committee described the FICZ as illegal and contrary to international law" (S. 21, p. 187)

That is, some 100 countries, or two-thirds of the international community of nations, have condemned the measure. This certainly did not contribute to the political or economic stability of the region, and it dimmed the prospects of an Anglo-Argentine understanding in the area of the dispute.

Argentina's position referred to earlier has not changed. And, obviously, any decision related to maritime jurisdiction implies prejudging the central issue, that is, sovereignty over the territories to which these jurisdictions belong. As for practical problems, the situation caused multiple difficulties, beginning with marking the limit between the waters that are undeniably Argentina's and those in dispute that both parties claim.

In summary, the necessity of involving the Argentine Republic in the decisions on the institutional future of the southern archipelagoes is an inevitability, dictated by the adequate exploitation of natural resources in the region. The political and economic difficulties have been set forth, and I will return to this theme in the final chapter. For the moment, I close with quotations from British political and academic circles, which all recognize Argentine participation as unavoidable and propose different alternatives for obtaining it.

ALTERNATIVE ARRANGEMENTS FOR
INVOLVING ARGENTINA PROPOSED BY
BRITISH POLITICAL AND ACADEMIC CIRCLES

Even during the armed conflict, with a considerable number of casualties on both sides, British political and academic circles understood that the silencing of their weapons was only one phase of the bilateral Anglo-Argentine controversy. It was not a solution. Rather, to use Walter Little's words, "The basic problem of who should exercise sovereignty over the islands remains as intractable as ever" (S. 14, p. 139).

Political circles.

If that is the reality of the political scenario, it should be no surprise that Francis Pym, who was the head of the Foreign Office during the din of battle, said of the accords with Argentina: "It would be wrong to close the door of any option which might be the best answer for the Islanders in the future" (S. 5, p. 89).

But before commenting on the alternatives bandied about in British political circles as solutions to the Malvinas question, I should briefly digress and examine the panorama of traditional groupings espousing them.

The views of the political parties. Walter Little has made a rather detailed analysis of the strategies of political parties in Great Britain with respect to the Malvinas. His evaluation follows:

> In general, Conservative sympathizers are more hardline than those of the Liberal and Social Democratic parties, who in turn are less conciliatory than Labour supporters. However, all groups are concerned about costs —a clear majority disbelieves that they are indefinitely sustainable—and all party groups are internally divided. The fact that around a third of Labour supporters are hardline while an equal proportion of their Tory counterparts are conciliatory is important because it blurs the message being sent to decision makers.

And he continues:

> Given the high centralized nature of the executive in Britain and the size of the present government's majority, it is inconceivable that any doubts the electorate might have impinge on policy-making. Indeed the reverse is more likely, for those who do not have reservations are divided as to the future . . . while the hard core of 30–40 percent who oppose compromise not only have a clear preference [the status quo] but also seem to feel strongly enough about it to make their views felt in the event of their being questioned. (S. 14, p. 145–146)

Crowning this global assessment of the political context, Little sinks his scalpel into the well-known political parties of the United Kingdom. Of the Conservative Party, currently in power, he says:

> Within it, there is a considerable dissent, at least at Westminster. Ministers, of course, toe the official line but not with any enthusiasm. On the back-benches there are roughly three groups with a clear view: those who seek to outdo the Prime Minister in the support to the Islanders; those who have reservations about the cost of the policy; and those who actively urge some accommodation with Argentina. (Ibid., p. 146)

Little then mentions the reasons why the hard line comes across as more coherent, while those favoring compromise are limited to requesting an opening of negotiations but have no clear idea of how the sovereignty dispute might be resolved.

As for the parties that today constitute the opposition (Labour and Social Democrat), Little believes that they have made no great contributions to the subject. They insist on talks but without any prior conditions as to the results. They do not maintain that the Islanders' wishes must be paramount, but they accept that they cannot be ignored either. Little concludes that the Liberals and the SDP (an offshoot of conservatism that by now has disappeared) have been more explicit than Labour in recognizing that the United Nations should be involved. (Ibid., p. 147)

In any event, it would be naive to hide that in all of the political parties, at the moment of decision, a negative component appears that impedes a just and rational approach to reaching an understanding with Argentina on the sovereignty issue. In the United Kingdom, as in any corner of the world, this emotional element is always present. Particularly—as in this case—when it has been stained with blood, professional politicians perceive "that the issue could generate popular nationalism which may work to their electoral disadvantage" (S. 4, p. 147).

These considerations are important because they serve to demystify certain interpretations of presumed radical changes in the British position in the event of a future administration of a political stripe different from the current one. They also shed light on reasons why, with few exceptions, parliamentarians who supposedly favor an arrangement with Argentina rarely speak up.

As to the necessity of involving Argentina in the institutional solution to the southern archipelagoes, I believe the words spoken more than five years ago by Labour's George Foulkes summarize the situation: "The inevitability of the talks with Argentina is conceded by the government and that only the timing and the decision about when they should start is what is in doubt" (S. 4, p. 29). As we shall see later, the attitude of Argentine President Carlos Menem served as a catalyst and precipitated bilateral meetings.

Alternative strategies for solution. The expert hand of Walter Little has guided us through the subtleties of the political parties. It is now appropriate to explore the approaches and the detailed proposals that partisan supporters have suggested in relation to the sovereignty dispute.

An interesting statement from the political milieu is the August 1984 report by the Committee on Latin America of the Foreign Affairs Panel of the Liberal Party. Although its head, Jack Speyer, clarifies that the document does not represent the political party's viewpoint, it is clear that the views expressed are valid for the purposes of this essay.

I will summarize his main ideas, which begin with a realistic and timely statement to the effect that there must be rapid progress toward a negotiated arrangement (S. 34, p. 4). In that context the report dedicates the entire final section to an analysis of what it calls alternatives to a solution. It lists the following: integration with the United Kingdom; incorporation into the Antarctic Treaty; status as a United Nations trusteeship; transfer to Argentina with a leaseback to Great Britain; condominium; and a sixth option, which is clearly the committee's preference. This option is autonomy for the Malvinas Islands in an association with Argentina, accompanied by international guarantees, noncompliance with which would automatically affect the ceding of sovereignty to Argentina.

The structure of autonomy or self-government of the islands—inspired by the Swedish-Finnish agreement on the Aland Islands—includes interesting elements:

- Conditional transfer of sovereignty to Argentina, which could designate a civilian governor; after a transition period, use of Argentine currency
- Full rights to the exploitation of natural resources by Argentina with the sole obligation to pay the Islanders a percentage of the revenues
- Local legislature directly elected and an executive council with the power to levy taxes and/or collect a percentage of the revenues from the exploitation of natural resources (oil, fishing, etc.)
- Its own flag, which would fly with the Argentine flag; two official languages; local authorities with the power to determine residence
- Dual nationality; demilitarization; freedom of religion; participation of two island representatives in the Argentine Congress
- Applicability of Argentine legislation subject to ratification by the local legislature
- Recognition of the rights and duties remaining to the United Kingdom for between five and ten years; rights to British fishing vessels; economic aid for the development of the islands and guarantees to those Islanders seeking to emigrate

The basic treaty would include a clause guaranteeing the intervention of the United Nations Security Council and eventual suspension of Argentine sovereignty in the event of any violation of the agreement. A final clause includes the concept of self-determination, leaving to the will of 75 percent of the Kelpers—expressed through a referendum—the rejection of some or all of the provisions of the agreement.

I mention this document in some detail for two reasons: it contains original ideas and it clearly demonstrates that there are British politicians today willing to seriously negotiate the issues of sovereignty over the islands.

Although not in the same depth with which I analyzed the above, I also examined seven different alternatives appearing in an article by the secretary of the Foreign Affairs Committee of the Bow Group—which does not officially represent the Conservative Party but in general reflects its opinions:

   i. To refer the question to the International Court of Justice
   ii. For both parties to grant independence to the Falkland Islands
   iii. For Britain to acknowledge Argentine sovereignty and to accept leaseback
   iv. For Britain to sell its interest to Argentina, full compensation being paid to the Islanders
   v. For Britain to cede West Falkland and retain East Falkland
   vi. To establish a condominium
   vii. To place the islands under trusteeship, whereby no nation would have sovereignty

Finally, the paper took a position in favor of a sophisticated arrangement for an international trusteeship, which I do not consider very realistic.

In the course of the investigation conducted by the Kershaw Committee, one of its members asked Dr. Little about the feasibility of the so-called "Andorra option" discussed in certain circles, "which means that both Argentina and Britain would merge their sovereignty and there would be joint sovereignty leaving the Falklands to self-government."

With respect to this option based on the autonomy of the islands, he obtained the following response: "That would run counter to Argentine claims to exclusive sovereignty, but I am not sure if that reaction is justified." He said that it had not been seriously discussed at the bilateral level. The Islanders had examined it on various occasions in the past, but had not followed through. "Yes, it is certainly one of the sorts of things that one would perhaps want to talk about if the communications existed," which was interpreted "that an Andorra situation might be a runner." (Ibid.)

Obviously the opinion in the Foreign Affairs Committee of the House of Commons is a qualified expression representing British political circles.

I need not reiterate here that it analyzed in its first draft report several options that mainly implied involving Argentina in the institutional framework.

Under the title "The Main Alternatives," the Kershaw Committee includes "the so-called leaseback option . . . , joint administration or pooling of sovereignty in a condominium or co-sovereignty arrangement." It concludes by stressing the advantages of a leaseback and asserting that "the passage of time may well make possible a reopening of discussions along these lines." (S. 6, p. xliii)

I leave it to the reader to decide whether all this stands as clear testimony from British political circles on the necessity of involving Argentina in the institutional solution to the Malvinas question.

Academic circles.

In the United Kingdom, the Malvinas question enjoyed a very low priority in government circles until the 1982 conflict, and intellectual circles proved no less indifferent. "The official neglect was paralleled by lack of academic interest, since few British studies on the Falklands had been published" (S. 13, p. 140).

It was the war that triggered an interest in the problem among British writers, both among political scientists and experts in international law. In spite of this flurry of activity, the nucleus of experts in academic circles remains small—and thus I have had to be somewhat repetitious in citing names. The method I use in this essay is nothing more than an uninterrupted series of commentaries and assessments by British writers. Thus, I could limit myself in this section to a review of the options quoted in previous chapters.

I cannot resist the temptation of citing here a thought, relevant to the purpose of this chapter, from each of those writers who have made major contributions to the subject:

- Malcolm Deas, on the usurpation of 1833: "This was part of our imperial expansion and we took a bit of their territory because it was of great naval importance" (S. 2, p. 137).
- Jeffrey Mhyre, on the best title: "Perhaps the islands are British by prescription and self-determination. More likely they belong to Argentina by uti possidetis acquisition of Spain's rights or by occupation of terra nullis" (S. 18, p. 35).
- Denzil Dunnett, on the supremacy of the principle of territorial integrity: "There is no point in not recognizing that the United Nations has on occasions allowed precedence over self-determination to other considerations, in particular territorial integrity" (S. 10, p. 425).

- Joan Pearce, on the area in the sovereignty controversy: "The current dispute is then limited in law to the Falkland Islands, South Georgia and the South Sandwich Islands, as indeed were the negotiations proposed to be held in July 1977 between Argentina and the United Kingdom" (*Negotiations,* S. 23, p. 5).
- Peter Beck, on the mistakes in British policy: "Including the political preference to manage rather than to resolve the dispute" (S. 21, p. 4) and the necessity of involving Argentina: "It has been argued that it is unrealistic to pursue a solution unless Argentina has been involved and has approved" (S. 13, p. 146).
- William Wallace, who adopted the opinion of a member of Parliament on the lack of political courage to confront the question: "The problem is that no government had the guts to direct British public attention to the need for the problem to be solved rationally" (S. 12, p. 4).
- C. R. Mitchell, with respect to the interest in finding a solution: "Divisible, sharable sovereignty is a starting assumption that leads in the direction of solutions from which both sides can gain . . . avoiding costs of continuing in confrontation and the risk of open conflict at some stage in the future" (S. 16, p. 21).
- Professor James Fawcett, whose close adhesion to the British cause does not prevent him from proposing that Argentina share the resources: "What I suggest is that the principles which the Antarctic Treaty embodies (suspension of sovereignty, sharing resources) could be usefully aimed at in a possible agreement" (S. 2, p. 143).
- Michael Stephen, on the approach of substantive negotiations: "The objective must be to find a modus vivendi without the loss of face, or of vital interests of either side (S. 15, p. 1).
- Walter Little, with respect to the essential element: "Technical solutions to the dispute abound . . . but until the will to embrace them exists they remain mere speculation" (S. 14, p. 155).

In these quotations, as in the "confessions" cited throughout this essay, British writers have been very clear. Every effort to summarize them runs the risk of detracting from the originality of their messages. Synthesis thus lies with the reader.

4

Some Factors to Take into Account for Future Negotiations

REFLECTIONS ON THE REFERENTIAL FRAMEWORK

In the preceding chapter we saw that the British recognize the necessity of involving Argentina in the institutional future of the Malvinas Islands and of the other southern archipelagoes that are the subject of the controversy over sovereignty.

This acceptance is not a gratuitous gesture nor is it the result of any British altruism, but rather emerges from the very roots of the conflict, which has persisted for over a century and a half without solution, whether through mutual agreement or through tacit or explicit consent to the de facto situation. As Jeane Kirkpatrick noted, for Argentina "this is not a sudden passion, but a long-sustained national concern that stretches back 150 years" (S. 21, p. 31).

By 1983, the members of the Committee of the House of Commons, when meeting under their mandate to examine the institutional future of the Malvinas, stated: "The British insistence on her claim to perpetual and nonnegotiable sovereignty over the islands . . . was not generally expected or accepted at the United Nations as the long-term outcome of the dispute" (S. 4, p. xxiii). And they certainly had doubts "about the desirability of maintaining sovereignty in perpetuity" (Ibid.).

This and other British statements dispel a hope cherished during the Thatcher administration: that the armed conflict of 1982 resolved the sovereignty dispute once and for all. Peter Beck acknowledges this too, saying: "The conflict restored British control over the islands but failed to resolve the longrunning sovereignty dispute" (S. 21, p. 169). Clearly, then, negotiations on the issue in dispute must be resumed some day, so that the case has a just solution that ensures the rights as well as the interests of the parties involved.

Regarding those rights, I believe that I have convincingly demonstrated, using the other party's own admissions, that the Argentine position is unquestionably solid. But the confused history of the southern archipelagoes underlines the political dimension peculiar to the Malvinas case, and a thorough investigation of the deep-seated causes becomes inevitable. It is this that leads me to analyze the scenario in which are set forth the dispute, its component factors, and the main actors and their vital interests, and to examine what these variables suggest for the negotiating process.

THE "SOUTH ATLANTIC" SCENARIO: FACTORS IN PLAY AND PRINCIPAL PLAYERS

From a political science viewpoint, the South Atlantic—where the three disputed archipelagoes lie—constitutes a geopolitical scenario with its own characteristics in the field of international relations. I begin my examination of this scenario by analyzing two primary factors: the strategic and the economic. Because of their deciding role in the past and their predictable future importance, I also examine the Islanders as a factor. I then complete my analysis with several conclusions regarding the principal players in the Malvinas scenario.

The strategic factor.

Successive British sources have left a historical record on the special strategic importance attached by the British to the Malvinas Islands.

As early as Johnson's pamphlet, quoted above, which dates from 1771, it is mentioned that the book on Anson's travels changed the vague interest that the islands aroused:

> Finding the settlement in Pepy's or Falkland's Islands recommended by the author as necessary to the success of our future expeditions against the coast of Chile, and as of such use and importance, that it would produce many advantages in peace and in war would make us the masters of the south sea.

He later adds: "That such a settlement may be of use in war, no man that considers its situation will deny." (S. 7, p. 10)

Years later, in a letter dated July 20, 1775, Lord Egmont, whose appointment as Lord of the Admiralty in 1763 was decisive in the raising of the settlement bearing his name on Saunders Island, stated: "This station . . . is undoubtedly the key to the whole Pacific Ocean." And after naming the Latin American countries bordering on the Pacific, he added: "It will render all our expeditions to those parts more lucrative to ourselves, most fatal to Spain and no longer formidable, tedious and uncertain in a future war." (S. 27, p. 117)

The islands were abandoned by the United Kingdom until, after decades of indifference, British interest in the Malvinas was revived, and the Colonial Office distributed a circular stressing the advantage of occupying the islands due to "the political reasons for obtaining possession of such an important station for our Naval Force" (Ibid., p. 118).

This circular was brought to the attention of John Murray, Secretary of War and the Colonies, who resolved to consult the Duke of Wellington. In a letter sent to him dated July 23, 1829, Murray included the strategic interest in occupying the islands "from a naval point of view."

Thus, a little later, on August 8 of that year, Minister Aberdeen sent a note to Parish, who was then chargé d'affaires in Buenos Aires, in which he said that, aware of the growing importance of the Malvinas Islands, the government of the United Kingdom believed to be highly desirable the possession of some safe point where its ships could be supplied and, if necessary, repaired. In the event that the United Kingdom found itself engaged in war in the Western Hemisphere, such action would be almost indispensable to a successful outcome. (Ibid., p. 122)

It was such concerns that prompted Parish to protest Argentine occupation of the islands, thus, as Beck says, "providing a foundation for action designed to give substance not only to Britain's 'just rights' but also its strategic, commercial and other interests, which included the Islands' perceived value as a secure naval station at a time of suspected French and American interest" (S. 21, p. 43).

Given the sequence of these diplomatic moves, there is no doubt that the strategic factor was what drove the British to seize the islands in 1833, without prejudice to the importance of the Malvinas to simple commercial navigation.

A century later, in the 1930s, which Beck calls a period of doubt and debate, "the legal and historical uncertainties, along with the continuing vital strategic and economic role of the Falklands, produced the consolidation of the traditional British policies" (S. 11, p. 15).

Taking from the internal memoranda closed to the public, which he did not hesitate to transcribe, Beck said that in the 1930s Gerald Fitzmaurice, legal adviser to the Foreign Office, recognized that the United Kingdom had categorically rejected the Argentine request in 1884 to submit the Malvinas question to international arbitration. The reason was that in view of the islands' considerable strategic value as a naval base, it did not want to gamble on an adverse decision.

During World War II also, the Malvinas proved useful to the British, as witnessed by the outcome of the battle off the Rio de la Plata with the

German pocket battleship *Graf Spee*. Beck notes that "during this period the Falkland Islands proved an 'important colonial possession' and policy interest for a global power like Britain" (S. 21, p. 93).

Now, the Islanders insist that the strategic value of their archipelago is undiminished, and during the conflict in 1982, Mrs. Thatcher herself, understandably, pointed to "the Islands' value as . . . the entrance to the Antarctic" (S. 21, p. 191).

In the midst of a war, one would hardly expect her to say the islands were of no strategic value. Be that as it may, and whatever the situation was in 1982, the fact of the matter is that as of today, the islands are of virtually no strategic value to anyone. Great Britain is no longer a global power. Not only that but the whole world situation has changed. The Cold War is over. The Soviet Union has collapsed. There are no further concerns about Soviet fleet strength or about the possibility of Soviet interdiction of the passages around either Cape Horn or the Cape of Good Hope.

As Beck notes, the islands were of great value to a power with a global presence—such as Great Britain used to have—but may be a drag now that it has ceased to be a global power with a far-ranging navy. Such "over-extended overseas commitments," he notes, "are no longer feasible" (S. 13, p. 146).

The economic factor.

We have seen that the economic factor became increasingly important to the British after the mid-1970s, exactly when the Organization of Petroleum Exporting Countries (OPEC) decided on a disproportionate rise in the prices of crude oil. This price increase threatened to destabilize the world economy and caused a race on the part of the developed countries toward new geological reserves of the valued hydrocarbon. The United Kingdom was no exception.

Peter Beck confirms this and says: "In fact John Callaghan [foreign minister from 1974 until April 1976 and prime minister from then until 1979] admitted that at this time he perceived the dispute partly through the eyes of the OPEC problem and thus an opportunity rather than a burden" (S. 21, p. 114: BBC lecture, "The Little Platoon," May 3, 1987).

The same author notes that this nourished Argentine suspicions that "the British were after the Islanders' oil" (Ibid.). He was correct, with the important limitation that Argentina—based on the position that illicit acts do not give rise to any rights—has always considered that all the oil in the area belonged to it.

Lord Shackleton's estimates of the extent of these resources in early 1976 are part of this political orientation. His report of that year only consolidated and "served as a catalyst in regard to the development of British policy through the appraisal of the South Atlantic's considerable economic potential" (S. 25, p. 47).

Proof of this is how the economic factor likewise filled the proposals from the Labour administration of that period (1978–1979), contained in the Rowlands paper, which I commented upon in some detail in Chapter 2.

Later, as we saw, and as British writers themselves admit, everything fell under an umbral cone because of blindness or lack of vision in their political circles. The efforts of Nicholas Ridley, Foreign Office negotiator, were futile. He favored reaching an understanding with Argentina and facilitating investment and economic cooperation in the area. However, "as with the fisheries, any proposal to prospect oil off the Falkland Islands themselves has been . . . blighted by the continuing impasse over sovereignty; thus the consequent political uncertainty has reduced the region's appeal to investors" (S. 9, p. 49).

From that point on, the United Kingdom, reined in by the Islanders' lobby, was left without a negotiating position. Emotions took the place of reason and buried the importance of the economic factor in the handling of bilateral negotiations.

Years later and after the armed conflict, the Kershaw Committee, in its first document (which was not approved), dredged up the old economic interest. In addition to the strategic considerations mentioned earlier, it said: "Finally it would defend the interest of the West in securing access to undersea resources in the region as well as those of Antarctica" (S. 4, p. xlviii).

I am of the opinion that the interests of the West in the resources of the area have never been in any danger. Naturally I maintain this because the Argentines—considering their ethnicity, their religion, their culture— are part of the West. The statement quoted is somewhat ambiguous and could seem ingenuous. If it claims to ensure access to resources behind Argentina's back, I do not think this is the case, it fundamentally being a question of the resources of the continental shelf.

But fortunately this is not the suggested approach, because the same report incorporates very positive recommendations as to negotiating the regulation and exploitation of the resources of the area with Argentina:

> We recommend that HM government should consider making a public announcement on the nonsovereignty issues which it is prepared to discuss with Argentina . . . including possibly the exploitation and regulation of the hydrocarbon and fisheries resources in the area of the Falkland and Dependencies, without prejudice to the territorial claim of the countries concerned in the area. (Ibid., p. xl, paragraph 99)

It would be dishonest to omit here a reference to the economic impact of the establishment of a fishing conservation zone by the United Kingdom in 1986. Licensing fishermen of different nationalities, and charging them for the right to dock for purposes of receiving supplies and transporting the catch to warehouses, has introduced new elements into the very evaluation of the political economy. The plentiful profits produced for the island community constitute a positive factor, but one that has been obscured because it has occurred "in spite of" Argentine rights and not "in the exercise of" those rights, expressed in an agreement with the Argentine Republic.

I believe that this negative impact on the Argentine cause should not be magnified. I am honestly of the opinion that Peter Beck's rationalization continues to be essentially valid: "The post-1986 fishing controversy proved essentially a function of the sovereignty problem, thereby implying that no particular aspect could be settled while the central issue was ignored" (S. 21, p. 192).

This is to say that the administration of fishing resources today in force in the waters of the Malvinas cannot be understood as a definitive arrangement. It is that way, among other reasons, because the measure is termed "provisional" and is not based on law. It responds moreover to a unilateral decision rather than to a negotiated decision, as the United Nations would like. On the contrary, not only has it been rejected by the other party, but it has also been repudiated by two-thirds of the member countries of the international community.

The islander factor.

For a better understanding of the point of view of the Islanders in the Malvinas scenario, let us first examine Walter Little's work on the socio-economic fabric of the island community:

> Despite its small size, its community is surprisingly diverse: Government employees, contract expatriates, Falkland Island Company employees, independent farmers, farm managers and labourers have distinct if overlapping interests. This is compounded by the differences between Stanley and camp residents, in income levels, education and personal and family reputations. It is not, then, so homogeneous a society as it might seem.

And he adds:

> Though privately often deeply critical of the British government . . . , the vast majority wish to see continued British administration. . . . Some would like more autonomy but always with the proviso of a British protective umbrella. (S. 14, p. 148)

However, let us remember learning from a Kelper that in 1980—during a visit by Nicholas Ridley—an appreciable majority of the population was willing to talk about the elements characterizing a leaseback. That is, it was just a matter of defining a period of time in which to transfer sovereignty to Argentina; the means for certain autonomy for the Islanders; guarantees as to their way of life, and so forth. Later this positive climate deteriorated because of the Islanders' obstinacy and, finally, it came to shrapnel and wounds, not only to the body but also to the spirit, which are the most difficult to heal.

So it was no surprise that when the members of the Kershaw Committee visited the islands in January 1983, Mr. Wallace of the Legislative Council and other prominent members of the island community proved uncompromising—to the point where they let it be known that, in the event of an agreement favorable to Argentina, it would be necessary to consider assuming the costs of relocating the Islanders and compensating their loss of land and other property.

It is probable that this very extreme attitude was a tactical position, based on prior complicity, that would not have been difficult to obtain in a small community. Of course, there were exceptions. In a much more balanced manner, Mr. Watt, a Kelper-designated adviser to the Kershaw Committee, said that with respect to a serious solution he thought:

> What the progress might be on the central issue depends on how one fudges or blurs the concept of sovereignty on the one hand and self-determination on the other. . . . A lot of proposals have been made . . . including of a leaseback kind. I imagine that most people would think that if the leaseback is long enough maybe that is something that could be looked at in due course. But, of course, it would require all sorts of guarantees about the way of life of the Islanders and so on . . . and it would also require some blurring of the word "sovereignty." . . . It does not look too promising at the moment, but I would not entirely rule it out. (S. 5, p. 4)

Another element, surely more intricate, is to overcome the anger aroused by the conflict, which has reinforced the Islander factor. The Kelpers are also more aware of their political clout and they exert it very coherently. They have strengthened their lobby which now includes the Falkland Islands Committee with headquarters in London and in the island capital; the Falkland Islands Association; and an active group of some 20 Members of Parliament representing all political parties.

The conflict, moreover, has permitted them to improve their status: They are now British citizens. It has also given them greater political autonomy—tempering the preceding crude colonial structure—and so the 1985 constitution increased their representation on the executive and legislative councils. After 1987, the licensing of fishing vessels produced considerable revenues, which gave the islands economic viability and increased the Kelpers' confidence in their future. (S. 21, p. 151)

It is true that, at the end of 1983, a lobby favorable to an understanding with Argentina was created—the South Atlantic Council—including members of Parliament, academics, and business professionals. Its objective, among others, is to seek a negotiated compromise, and it suggests that sovereignty must be on the agenda to be discussed, without any preconceptions. Several meetings have been held, and apparently the council has created a climate of better understanding among its members in both countries. But not much more can be expected of it.

In any event, I accept that the Islander factor is one of the most complex variables of the Malvinas scenario. Perhaps Little offers the key to it when he says that the desires of the Islanders must be honored but are not paramount "and there is no reason to suppose that they would not welcome a change" (S. 14, p. 149).

This assessment implies accepting at least the inconsistency of the status quo and the fact that some level of accommodation with Argentina is inevitable. In summary, there is a varied spectrum of attitudes, including island voices that recognize the necessity of involving Argentina in the future institutional solution. On the other hand, it must not be forgotten that the Islanders are not an independent party to the Anglo-Argentine bilateral negotiations, although that does not detract from the undeniable importance of their opinion.

One unforeseen event has had an impact upon the island community. Pursuant to the policy of economic deregulation, a new Argentine law on fishing was adopted in 1992 and has resulted in the sudden reduction of Kelper income. The chartering of foreign ships, permitting an increase in the Argentine catch, has reduced the 1992–1993 fishing revenues in the islands to an estimated maximum of 13.7 million pounds, nearly half of the figure expected from fishing licenses. In an article entitled "A Close Look at the Crisis," *The Penguin News*, the local newspaper, also reported that there would be important cuts in the budget and operating expenses of the islands.

This event was the subject of bilateral negotiations in a meeting of the South Atlantic Fisheries Commission held in Buenos Aires in October 1993. But previously, the Argentine foreign minister had said in a press conference that his country would not make a political issue out of a squid catch, and that the interest of the government was in rational fishing and conservation practices. The meeting of the commission confirmed this view, and a joint statement issued in London on November 1, 1993, mentioned, among other things, that in order to ensure the conservation of the Illex (a species of squid) during the 1994 fishing season, the Argentine government would authorize only catches of no more than 220,000 metric tons and would allow a maximum of 50 foreign flag vessels to fish for the squid.

This limitation was in relation to the maritime area between 45° and 60° S. latitude, with no distinction between the Argentine EEZ and the disputed 200-mile zone. But in another joint statement made in London and Buenos Aires on December 30, 1993, both governments extended the accord to the maritime area defined in the annex to the November 28, 1990, joint statement (Appendix 4 of this book).

As a consequence, when authorizing a catch in accordance with the November 1993 conditions, they are jointly putting an end to the temporary ban, and they do so in a zone corresponding to the Malvinas's 200-mile claim.

Despite this change on negotiating positions, the Islanders have cause to consider the consequences of the exploitation of nonrenewable resources in the seabed because, quite apart from logistical aspects, every private oil company (regardless of nationality) will prefer to collaborate with Argentina because of the greater security of its investment.

The actors in the Malvinas scenario.

Evaluating the Malvinas scenario as a political scientist, I conclude first that there are two principal players, Argentina and the United Kingdom—that is, the countries confronting each other in the controversy over sovereignty.

When I analyzed earlier the influence of the strategic factor on the dispute, I concluded that for the United Kingdom it currently played a role within the Atlantic military alliance. Furthermore, it is unquestionable that, since the creation of the alliance in 1949, the major burden of that responsibility falls on the United States of America, with the peculiarity that this responsibility increases with an issue centered in the South Atlantic. Consequently, it is inevitable when speaking of the strategic aspects of the Malvinas to include the leader of the strategic Western bloc, which in my judgment constitutes the third principal player in the southern scenario.

For those students of realpolitik, the principal players are those occupying the dominant positions in a defined international scenario and, normally, they set the courses of action and implement them. These principal players are also closely interested in the case, and consequently they usually participate in selecting the courses of action and they share and support them. Certainly, other actors exist that I could term peripheral or marginal, but although they can accompany a determined course of action and even support it with collateral means (diplomatic, financial, etc.), they are not determinative. Hence, I will exclude them from the present analysis.

We shall now see how the United States has become fully deserving of the classification I have assigned to it as a direct actor in the Malvinas scenario. I have already shown that the great democracy of the North has been involved in the history of the islands from the beginning. To a certain extent, it is appropriate to conclude that the arrogant incursion of the frigate USS *Lexington* and its commander's declaration that the islands belonged to no government "paved the way"—as Malcolm Deas recognizes—for the British usurpation of 1833.

Furthermore, U.S. diplomacy encouraged the consolidation of this act of British imperialism by not accepting the application of the Monroe Doctrine to the Malvinas. Proclaimed on December 2, 1823, it incorporated for the first time the Latin American countries into the balance of power in force at the time. Peter Beck notes in an article that this exclusion is stated in the answer transmitted to the Argentine government in 1841, where it is argued that the United Kingdom had exerted a claim based on events predating the Monroe Doctrine.

Beck correctly states that the current British emphasis on post-1833 arguments gives a certain justification to deductions by Argentina—supported by a writer of the stature of Julius Goebel—that "in reality Britain's action in 1833 represented a breach of the Monroe Doctrine, even if in reality the U.S. lacked the power to enforce it against Britain" (S. 11, p. 20).

But these events occurred during a historical period different from the setting of the dispute since the 1960s. In relation to the politico-diplomatic channeling of the sovereignty controversy since then (and until April 1982), I cite the opinion of Undersecretary John Ure of the Foreign Office:

> The United States have told us on a number of occasions that they have studiously avoided, over the years, taking a position on the sovereignty issue. That is not the same as we have seen; they were prepared to take a very firm and positive position on the Falklands conflict but they have not taken a position on the sovereignty dispute. (S. 4, p. 33)

With the 1982 conflict over—and the United States chiefs of staff were clear as to the extent of the real importance of their cooperation with the United Kingdom—the draft report of the Kershaw Committee set forth a sort of United States dilemma around the Anglo-Argentine dispute. It reads as follows: "It is this inter-American dimension to the dispute, which appears to lie behind the reluctance of the USA to become publicly identified with the British position." And it infers:

> For the moment the USA appears to have accepted the need for a cooling-off period and has indicated its preference for a peacefully negotiated solution as well as offering its good offices. But the USA has a need to be on good terms with Argentina as well as Britain. (S. 4, p. xlvi, paragraph 5.1)

This document, taking up the idea of the good offices offered by the United States, comes to the conclusion that the latter "has indicated its willingness to become involved not only through its actions as the conflict unfolded, but also for the future" (Ibid., p. xlix, paragraph 6.14). And it concludes, "it is clear that any settlement of the Falklands dispute will require American compliance and goodwill" (Ibid., p. L, paragraph 6.17).

Exactly as Jeane Kirkpatrick, Permanent Representative to the United Nations, emphasized, "Britain and Argentina had a stake in the Falklands, but in many ways the U.S. had the largest stake of all" (S. 21, p. 14). What is manifest in the texts transcribed is that in granting to the leader of the Atlantic Alliance a principal role directly in the Malvinas scenario, I am not alone. Moreover, Kirkpatrick's commentary leads us to believe that, perhaps in colloquial terms, she is implying the necessity of recognizing the existence of vital national interests in the area. The approach is relevant and deserves consideration, so I will return to it at the end of this essay.

THE CONDITIONINGS OF OPPORTUNITY: THE STAGES OF THE NEGOTIATIONS

In politics—and international politics is no exception—timing is fundamental. Anglo-Saxons are masters at timing as a formidable component of any course of action to be undertaken. This variable of timeliness is in my opinion an essential ingredient in the parameters today framing the handling of the Malvinas matter. It suggests approaching the different aspects of this complex case in light of the elements that condition them, which determines convenience, or even more, political interest, in passing through stages, step by step, as the United Kingdom has repeatedly proposed. The fact that this manner has been suggested by the British—which is one of the principal players—is not the only, nor even the most important, reason it is highly recommendable.

The 1982 armed conflict obviously left open wounds. Without going into laborious studies of the emotional world of Margaret Thatcher, her personal decision was to consider the Malvinas question as a closed case after Argentina's military surrender. In this connection, we should also mention the words of Walter Little, who after confirming that the United Kingdom's inflexible policy during the first years was "her creation," added: "The stridency of her language [opposed to any inclusion of the subject of sovereignty] has to some degree obscured her real position . . . that she has become a prisoner of her past action and the rhetoric that has followed them." And somewhat mercilessly he concludes: "For her to change policy now would be tantamount to admitting that she had let British troops die in vain." (S. 14, p. 147)

Although inexplicably it has never been made public by an Argentine source, today it is well known that the prime minister's posture went further than the obstruction of any inclusion of the subject of sovereignty.

The position of the Thatcher administration during its first few years was to claim that President Alfonsín's Argentina should accept—in the terms of reference that framed the talks—that sovereignty be expressly excluded. This is not my own interpretation, but comes from British sources.

It should be considered that at this first postconflict stage, Argentina made public on several occasions its political will to negotiate with an open agenda, without any agreement from the British side. The dialogue between Lord Kershaw and Lady Young, the secretary of state of the Foreign Office, is revealing. The head of the Committee of the House of Commons stated in this connection:

> The position appeared to be that Argentina were offering negotiation on an open agenda basis, in which nothing was specifically excluded, whilst Her Majesty's government wished the question of sovereignty to be specifically excluded.

And Secretary Young confirmed that position:

> Sovereignty involves the exclusive right to exercise state authority within a territory . . . and we have said . . . that we have no doubt about our sovereignty over the Falkland Islands. . . . We therefore said that we were not prepared to discuss sovereignty. (S. 5, p. 134)

In a similar vein, Kershaw questioned Francis Pym, reproaching him by asking, "Do you think it is reasonable to expect the Argentine government to attend discussions from which sovereignty is excluded?" The former foreign minister justified the position because of "the completely illegal and universally condemned invasion, and of course that does alter things and it is a very, very serious development indeed." However, he immediately let it be understood that the passage of time would permit a more flexible position. (S. 5, p. 87)

I share Lord Kershaw's opinion that the British excuse, referred to above, was completely unreasonable and could not have been accepted by any Argentine government. In politics there are nuances that raise insurmountable obstacles, and the Argentine position requiring an open agenda was, within the approach then adopted by "Palacio San Martín," a point of no return. The basis proposed by Argentina was so on the mark that Lord Henderson, at the time ambassador in Washington, commented, "I think that is a good basis upon which to approach this subject" (S. 5, p. 59).

Repeated indirect contacts in New York, through the Secretary-General of the United Nations, or off-the-record negotiations by officials of Washington's Department of State, did not significantly alter the scenario. These contacts did, however, permit greater knowledge of the respective positions and may have paved the way to later agreements.

The rise of Carlos Saúl Menem to power in June 1989 was to permit the subject to be placed under a different "prism." In the first place, the mere fact of having won the presidency through an exemplary democratic race weakened the argument of British hard-liners that Argentina offered no guarantees of not reverting to its authoritarian ways of recent years, including the repression of human rights. In the second place, because by late 1988 the United Kingdom—which had unilaterally repealed commercial and financial restrictions enacted during the conflict—began seriously suggesting to its partners in the European Community that Argentine revoke its own restrictions. At the same time, it advocated the initiation of a process toward the reestablishment of bilateral relations across the board.

Among its partners in the European Community were countries with close ties to the Argentine government, such as Spain and Italy, and Mitterrand's France, which maintained especially good relations with the Alfonsín administration. These governments urged the two adversaries toward more flexible positions, as did the United States.

But above all—and it would be inexcusable not to emphasize it—President Menem's political courage became part of the Malvinas scenario. Leaving aside any short-term speculations, he set for the Argentine Foreign Ministry a course of action that, taking into consideration exogenous conditioning factors, accepted the provisional freezing of substantive discussions on sovereignty.

It is difficult to analyze agreements that are still so recent and that in many cases constitute only a framework for future action. Fortunately, they have been openly discussed and have appeared in public documents, which allows me to make a preliminary evaluation like any other ordinary Argentine citizen familiar with the subject.

The meetings held in Madrid in October 1989 and in February 1990 crystallized the launching of a new stage in the century-old conflict with the United Kingdom. It led to the reestablishment of diplomatic relations between the two countries and to the elimination of the aftermath of armed conflict, particularly the Argentine economic restrictions referred to above, and to the lifting of the Protection Zone established by the United Kingdom in November 1982. Mutual trust was being reestablished, thus improving the climate for new understandings.

Although that was the objective and the Argentine government has recognized that it had accepted postponement of discussions of the substantive issue, in effect a classic approach to negotiations with the United Kingdom was put into effect: discussions on the basis of a reciprocal reservation of the respective positions on the subject of sovereignty. These positions remained thus "protected" by the "sovereignty umbrella," whatever initiative or proposal might be placed on the table.

The United Kingdom dropped its intolerable demand that the sovereignty theme be expressly excluded. The very application of the "umbrella" in question implies the acceptance by both parties of the existence of a controversy over sovereignty, which the document adopted at the first meeting extended to the three archipelagoes (Malvinas, South Georgia, and South Sandwich), wisely including the disputed area as consecrated in 1977. The negotiators, moreover, were sagacious in avoiding other obstacles (the cessation of hostilities), and they were prudent in postponing more complex agreements. These included anything related to fishing, which is inexorably linked to the resolution of the main issue.

In Madrid, an agreement on fishing conservation (Madrid III) was later signed which, despite its limited objective, confirms my preceding assessment. I will return to it in the final chapter.

SOVEREIGNTY AS A SET OF JURISDICTIONS SUSCEPTIBLE TO SEPARATE AGREEMENT AND NEGOTIATION

Walter Little reflects my judgment well: "Sovereignty has proved to be a major stumbling block because each side has taken sovereignty to be indivisible and absolute, that is something to be enjoyed to the full or not at all" (S. 14, p. 144).

With certain reservations Little's assessment is basically correct. Peter Beck reflects the same view:

> The basic obstacle in the way of agreement is, however, that both governments, while anxious to settle, are imprisoned by history—that is, by past pronouncements and obligations. Thus the British government is restrained by a commitment to respect the principle of self-determination as well as by the unchanging view of the Islanders. In turn, the manipulation of the dispute for both domestic and international purpose prevents Argentine acceptance of anything short of sovereignty. (S. 13, p. 147)

The average person will wonder what "absolute sovereignty" is or what accepting "a little less" means. A few brief clarification of the significance of sovereignty should be made here.

The conceptualization of the term "sovereignty."

Conceptualizing the term "sovereignty" is not an easy task. Karl Strupp maintained in his time that few words had caused such confusion, and later Charles Rousseau asserted that no writer to date had introduced a general theory of sovereignty (Strupp, "Les règles du droit de la paix," Rec. des cours, V, 47, 1934, p. 491; Rousseau, *Droit International Public*, 1953, N. 241, note 1).

I believe that much of the confusion derives from the existence of several doctrinal currents. I think it will clear the way if we accept that the absolutist theory, although it has its followers, constitutes an abstraction detached from any political or legal reality whose only value is historical. Let us observe, however, in Little's reflection, quoted above, the extent to which "absolute" continues to qualify the term.

The legal gap concerning a general theory of sovereignty to which Rousseau alluded persists, and the confusion is not less than before. But even so, if we accept along with Frankowsky ("L'idée de la souveraineté dans les relations internationales," *Revue de Droit International*, vol. 12, pp. 499–506) that international law includes the experiences of nations expressed in a system of norms, we have only to manipulate this concept molded by the secular practices of states and which, as is well known, is at the center of our drama.

Twenty years ago I made an effort to conceptualize the term sovereignty. I thought then and ratify now that sovereignty is essentially a title by virtue of which international law recognizes that a state has exclusive domain over a set of jurisdictions constituting its internal order and its international presence. At that time, I also defined its distinctive aspects, but I think that what I have already said is sufficient for the purposes of the task at hand. It is enough to break down a bit the previous conceptualization.

It should be clear in the first place that we are dealing with jurisdictions, in principle of an infinite variety because they include everything that is not prohibited by the general principles of international law, which in reality expressly recognizes in the state only a limited number. Let me clarify too that some jurisdictions depart from the discretional field of the original holder having been "regulated" by bilateral or multilateral compromises. In this respect, and given the evolutionary nature of the practices of states in the international arena, it can be stated today that in principle nothing is sacrosanct. These are exclusive jurisdictions of the state, which like any holder of anything, can do with them whatever its vision and its national interests suggest: surrender them, alienate them, exchange them for something else, transfer them, lease them—in whole or in part, temporarily or permanently. The respective jurisdictions can be alienated or their exercise may be suspended by the original holder, who transfers them to another state or interstate organization, or exercises them through joining in the collective will of such an organization. Of course, above all, it is implicit that the state is a unit of power, which permits it to regret having given something up and lets it revoke its relinquishment, whether or not it did so as part of its international responsibility.

But what should be clear is that it is as much a sovereign act of a State when it cedes jurisdiction as when it recovers it, if in either case it is an act of its own free will expressed in function of its national interests. Does not the current context offer us the example of important countries of the so-called First World—among them the United Kingdom—that have ceded their exercise of sovereign jurisdiction to an organization (the European Community) without anyone's doubting that this was carried out in the national interest?

At this point, and in spite of the complexity, I trust I have armed the lay reader with the information necessary for understanding the observations that follow and that are offered as closure to this book.

The sovereign jurisdictions integrating the "Malvinas Question." Theoretical methods of negotiation.

Few British citizens and probably no Argentine will admit ignorance of what *ratione materiae* implies, from a substantive point of view, for the Anglo-Argentine sovereignty dispute in the South Atlantic. I am convinced nonetheless that few are really familiar with it. In the first section I clarify this, giving it a novel introduction that seems useful to the objectives of this essay.

As to the area of substantive bilateral negotiations, I comment in the following section on some original alternatives for dealing with the question. Although it is not now a matter of reflecting the other party's "confession," I will not refrain from quoting here new assessments by British officials or academics, which, because they come from compatriots of those seated at the other side of the table, are always of interest.

The area of bilateral negotiations: A vision separated from its components. From the point of view of successive Argentine governments, there is no doubt that the controversy with the United Kingdom includes sovereignty over the three southern archipelagoes already mentioned repeatedly in this work: the Malvinas, the South Georgias, and the South Sandwich Islands.

As for the British side, it cannot be said that there has been the same coherence. But in the last few years one can deduce that they have accepted that the dispute goes beyond the Malvinas and includes the other archipelagoes. This appears expressly and clearly in various documents and attitudes:

- As reported by the Kershaw Committee, in the mandate to negotiate agreed to in April 1977 and duly communicated to the United Nations: "The UK agreed that the question of sovereignty over South Georgia and the South Sandwich Islands would be considered alongside the sovereignty of the Falkland Islands themselves" (S. 4, p. xlii, point 5.2).

- From the "mixed approach" proposed by Secretary of State Ted Rowlands, referred to in Chapter 2, which contained a series of initiatives on cooperation in the so-called Dependencies (FID).
- The administrative subordination that determines, as Professor Fawcett states, that "the basic law of the Dependencies is the law of the Falkland Islands, which is not entirely the same as English law" (S. 2, p. 140). This creates a firm link among the three archipelagoes, whose future might not be similar but which must be negotiated as a whole.
- The recent Madrid Accord of November 1989, which places the three archipelagoes—without distinguishing among them—under the umbrella of sovereignty, with a reciprocal reservation of the respective positions in the area subject to dispute.

Now, if the area in controversy includes (i) the territories of the three archipelagoes, and obviously their respective maritime jurisdictions, including in each case (ii) the territorial seas, (iii) the Exclusive Economic Zone (EEZ) with its fishing resources, and (iv) the continental shelf with nonrenewable resources on its surface and in its depths, then even if we lump the territories (i) and territorial seas (ii) together as a single unit, there would still be three types of units or interests (i, iii, and iv) in each of the three archipelagoes. On a theoretical plane, if we decided to segregate, separate the corresponding sovereign jurisdictions, we would find ourselves, mathematically, with nine subareas to be placed on the table at the bilateral negotiations and, hypothetically, they could each be the object of a different solution.

I repeat that this is only a theoretical exercise. Maritime jurisdictions normally correspond to the coastal state and, in principle, cannot be separated from the territories. But anything is possible for the sovereign will of the holders of those rights, and it is sufficient to note that in the Beagle treaty, the maritime jurisdictions of Argentina in the South Atlantic are defined by an imaginary line and not by terra firma.

C. R. Mitchell, a British writer from the City University of London, in a work on alternative approaches to the subject of sovereignty in the Malvinas matter, deals with these variables and mentions that one possibility is to divide the area in dispute "so both parties retain absolute authority within an agreed portion of the disputed territory" (S. 16, p. 19). In fact, this is the alternative that would be applied when Michael Stephen, of the Bow Group, among other options, spoke of separating the two principal islands and assigning sovereignty to each of the parties to the dispute, the "British to cede West Falkland and retain East Falkland" (S. 15, p. 10). If we must accept that this is another conceivable separation, our theoretical exercise based on Pythagorean theorems results in 12 subareas subject to negotiation.

An approach detached from the sovereign jurisdictions involved. Up to this point I have worked exclusively with a geographic or physical separation of the components forming the area in dispute. Certainly my conceptualization of sovereignty authorizes me to believe that other means exist for "separating" the sovereign jurisdictions inherent to the islands.

In reality, it is this approach to which Mitchell adheres when he affirms that there are other ways of sharing such jurisdictions and, consequently, there exists "an almost infinite set of solutions based on some negotiated division of rights and responsibilities" (Ibid., p. 20). And he includes some possible examples:

1. Divide sovereignty over the territory and over the people: "Citizens of country *Y* with the right to retain their way of life provided this way of life is commensurate with what the government and the people of country *X* regard as the reasonable long-term use of land and other territorial resources."

2. As more complex forms of separating the sovereign jurisdictions, he mentions: "Joint citizenship as opposed to being citizens of one country with the right to live on what is formally the territory of another; disassociation of jurisdictions as to security (internal and external which are assigned respectively to two different states); agreement about local autonomous government in the area, with rights to send elected representatives to one or both national (Argentine) assemblies." (Ibid., p. 21)

And Mitchell finally concludes: "Divisible, sharable sovereignty is a starting assumption that leads in the direction of solutions from which both sides can gain" (Ibid.).

Peter Beck also speaks at length on a series of options. In examining the one he calls "shared dual sovereignty," which in his example leads to an almost autonomous local administration, of the Andorra type, he mentions that the Argentine government (of the Radical Party) indicated its willingness to accept a reasonable degree of autonomy for the Islanders "even if this solution requires acceptance of something less than full sovereignty" (S. 21, p. 152).

He notes in this connection the constitutional clauses that would authorize formulas of autonomy for the Malvinas and mentions a declaration on the subject by the Argentine government in February 1985. If we add to these relevant factors those resulting from the proposals and alternatives for a solution to the dispute, which I commented on above when referring to the attitude of the political circles, I consider that I have set forth the essential concepts to ensure a correct reading of my concluding observations.

5

Reflections in the Form of an Epilogue: The Key to the Enigma

THE LEGAL APPROACH: THE MALVINAS QUESTION AND INTERNATIONAL LAW

In Chapter 1 I demonstrated that the British have admitted the weakness of their claims to sovereignty over the Malvinas Islands. I showed in the next chapter that these acknowledgments are most clearly expressed in a series of initiatives and proposals that the United Kingdom—formally or in the course of contacts or negotiations—submitted to the Argentine Republic. I judge these to contain implicit admissions of Argentine rights to the disputed archipelagoes—admissions that notably strengthen Argentina's legal position. And we should not forget that even in the nineteenth century, the British considered that position to be so formidable that they rejected the Buenos Aires government's proposal to submit the dispute over the sovereignty of the Malvinas to arbitration (1884–1888), obviously fearing an adverse decision, as Gerald Fitzmaurice, legal adviser to the Foreign Office, acknowledged with absolute candor some years later in a confidential document that has now become public (S. 11, p. 16).

It must be acknowledged that experts in international law will not corroborate the legal validity of the documentation found in internal departmental or interdepartmental reports. The same is true of some of the proposals commented upon above—the Rowlands case among others—which came under the protection of the reservations of rights (sovereignty umbrella), reducing their probative importance. Nonetheless, I am persuaded that, after the conflict of 1982, documentation of great legal significance was made available, all of it in favor of the Argentine cause.

The same is true of the documentation produced officially and publicly by the British government, such as the Franks Report—in connection with the proposed solutions bandied about by the United Kingdom—and the results of the investigation carried out by the House of Commons. Both permit not only the formulation of an Argentine legal case but also the dismissal of the British case to title to the islands—this through application of the doctrine of "estoppel," which encompasses that fundamental principle of civil law: *One party's own confession relieves the other party from the onus of proof.*

Not in vain, the British line of argument is confined to the continuity of its (de facto) administration of the islands and to the application of the principle of self-determination, whose invalidity I have already demonstrated. The British, in short, simply have no case—certainly none that would stand up in court.

In the context of international law, one last reflection remains: Did the Argentine occupation of the islands in 1982 modify the indisputable supremacy of its claims to sovereignty over the islands? And in answer, we have already quoted the legal adviser to the Foreign Office before the Kershaw Committee that no, legally, nothing was changed.

I will not go into a discussion of the armed conflict of 1982, because obviously that would be inconsistent both with the methodology of this work, which has been to rely on British sources, and with its declared purpose of looking toward the future. I will restrict myself to two very brief commentaries, both of which are relevant to the analysis of this case in the context of international law.

First, it is certainly questionable whether Argentina—given its claims to the islands, its willingness to resolve the case according to law through its request for international arbitration, its fruitless claims for a period of 150 years, and its good faith in negotiating for more than 15 years—could technically "invade" its own territory and be termed an aggressor. This assessment without a doubt prompted Jeane Kirkpatrick, a distinguished U.S. specialist in political science, and at the time U.S. permanent representative to the United Nations, to state on television, "I do not believe that Argentina, given the fact that it had a lasting claim to the sovereignty of the Falklands, could be said to be committing aggression by occupying them" (Ambassador Henderson, S. 5, p. 53). This evaluation of the event is important because, according to Article 51 of the United Nations Charter, aggression is the trigger that sets in motion the mechanism of legitimate individual (or collective) defense. And it was this article that the United Kingdom invoked to send into battle the most powerful fleet assembled since World War II.

Second, the rejection by UN member states of the use of or threat to use force, as stated in Article 2, paragraph 4 of the Charter—which according to British legal advisers is principally why the Argentine occupation of 1982 is illegal and their own occupation of 1833 legal—should not be interpreted in isolation from other provisions of the instrument cited. Among them, paragraph 3 of the same article concerns the peaceful resolution of conflicts, which is given equal priority. The obligation to seek, through negotiation, resolution to conflicts, when they can threaten international peace and security, is expressly contemplated in Article 33 of the Charter. This is logical, because the reverse would mean that if the adverse party who profits de facto from a dispute does not negotiate or does not do so in good faith, the other party would be unable to pursue its claim.

This is what happened to Argentina in the Malvinas case, as I demonstrated with the help of the Franks Report. The United Kingdom from 1981 forward had no negotiating position and limited itself to "buying time." In the Malvinas question, the obligation to negotiate, which takes on a permanent character as long as the dispute exists, is all the more valid as the generic norm cited has been reaffirmed repeatedly in pronouncements by the United Nations General Assembly expressly requiring it of both parties. According to some experts in international law, noncompliance with the relevant resolutions can mean the party is guilty of arbitrariness and abuse of law, exposing it to consequences derived from legal sanctions (Professor E. Lauterpacht in an advisory opinion of the International Court of Justice [ICJ], dated July 7, 1955, *Reports,* 1955, p. 120).

I think these reflections on the soundness of the Argentine position in the context of international law are worthy of consideration, not because I think that the resolution of this complex case can come through the law— the United Kingdom will not want to run the risk of an adverse ruling any more today than in the nineteenth century—but because I believe Argentine willingness to pursue such a solution shows how confident it is of its position. Hopefully, too, the Argentine example may encourage the British toward a willingness to seriously negotiate the issue.

THE POLITICAL APPROACH: BILATERAL NEGOTIATION

The players and their vital interests.

Since the United Nations decisions, the instrument chosen by the principal parties to the dispute is direct negotiations. In such negotiations, political factors weigh more heavily than those of a juridical nature. The most basic of all has to do with what each party regards as its national interests. Let us, then, briefly review what would seem to be each party's interests in the case of the Malvinas:

Argentina. Leaving aside the question of national pride and the emotional need to address a wrong done to it 130 years ago, Argentina has both strategic and economic interests in the area, with the latter by far the most important.

The strategic considerations do not flow from any Argentine need for naval bases in the Malvinas; rather, Argentina is among the countries claiming territory in Antarctica, and the eastern border of Argentina's sector is a line drawn from the disputed southern archipelagoes. Its claims in Antarctica, in other words, are related to its claims to sovereignty over the islands, though not inextricably so.

Of greater interest to Argentina is the sensible and profitable exploitation of the natural resources in the maritime space stretching from the coast of Patagonia to 200 miles beyond the islands, with all that implies in terms of conservation and exploration. In the latter context, drilling really should begin immediately as the only means of determining the extent and the nature of the hydrocarbon deposits.

United Kingdom. The United Kingdom's principal interest in the Malvinas, as we have seen, was initially of a strategic nature. Now that it is no longer a global power with a far-reaching navy, it really has no strategic need for bases in the islands. That interest was replaced, however, by one of an economic nature as a consequence of the energy crisis of 1975. Great Britain, like Argentina, has an interest in exploiting hydrocarbon deposits in the seas around the islands, if such deposits are found there and if exploitation is technically feasible. Those questions will not be answered for some time, however, and even if they are answered in the affirmative, effective exploitation would require agreement and cooperation with Argentina.

Stages of negotiations:
Some reflections on their characteristics.

The international community and the Argentine people expect that in the not too distant future bilateral negotiations on the substantive issue of the Malvinas can be resumed. We should not expect, at least for the time being, spectacular statements or actions to advance the process begun in 1989. For the time being, the Madrid agreements offer a positive framework and encourage hope for the future, particularly the last accord reached in November 1990 (Madrid III).

Let us focus attention on this one because the steps taken until then— formal cessation of hostilities, elimination of economic restrictions, lifting of the Exclusion Zone, and reestablishment of diplomatic relations at the ambassadorial level—all indicate a successful diplomatic effort to take bilateral relations back to their status prior to the armed conflict of 1982. But, as the Argentine government has recognized, they are tangential to the dispute over sovereignty.

On November 28, 1990, at the third meeting held in the Spanish capital, a joint declaration was signed on the conservation of fishing resources. This assumed a sort of Anglo-Argentine administrative body. But perhaps the most important aspect of this agreement is the maritime zone to which it applies. That area extends from the Conservation and Administration Zone declared by the British government in 1986 to the 200 miles of the Exclusive Economic Zone (EEZ) of the Malvinas to the east—that is, a jurisdiction belonging to the islands that has nothing to do with the EEZ of the continental Argentine coastline, as shown in Appendix 4.

The document cited creates a Fishing Commission of the South Atlantic with a series of functions, whose recommendations will be adopted "by mutual agreement." This forum held its first meeting in Buenos Aires in May 1991 and considered a program (fishing fleet operations, harvest information, fishing efforts) that assumes joint patrolling of the waters. It also recommended to the governments of both countries that a temporary ban on commercial fishing be declared in the area as an adjunct to the above-mentioned declaration. Further, the participants also decided on an evaluation of technical aspects with a view toward joint scientific research in the National Institute of Fishing Research and Development of Mar del Plata.

The second meeting of the commission took place in London on December 4 and 5 of the same year. The project was ratified and it was decided that during the week preceding the third meeting of this group, scheduled for May 1992, Argentine and British scientists would convene in Mar del Plata to draw up the program. The complete ban on commercial fishing was extended for another year beginning December 26, 1991. It is to be hoped that when the prohibition is lifted, fishing will be authorized by the same Commission, and that licenses required as a consequence will also be granted by a bilateral organization.

On November 22, 1991, measures referring, for the first time, to nonrenewable resources in the area were announced simultaneously in the capitals of both countries—which proves there were prior contacts. As is its custom, the British Foreign Office included in a press communiqué the minister of state's statement to Parliament. In it, he noted that rights over the continental shelf were recovered on October 29, 1986 (referring to a paragraph of the document on fishing from that year), and he said that he had been in contact with the government of the Malvinas to instruct it to "take the necessary legislative measures which would allow the exercise of the Crown's rights over the seabed and the floor of the continental shelf surrounding the islands." He also announced that the Legislative Council of the islands would be presented with an order called "the 1991 Law of the Continental Shelf" which, when it becomes effective, will permit seismic surveys in defined areas of the continental shelf, under license.

Argentina, for its part, issued a declaration promulgating Law (Act) 23.968 on the baselines of the Argentine coast from which the country measures its maritime space. This is fully applicable to the totality of insular and continental coast, including the Malvinas Islands, the South Georgia Islands, and the South Sandwich Islands. It refers to the legislation on the seismic surveys that the British government will allow. It also says that the Argentine government "does not accept nor does it consent to the jurisdiction which the British government attributes to itself," and that the areas mentioned are in dispute, as the United Nations recognizes. In the communiqué to which we refer, the British reject these declarations.

The statements of both governments mention that they place a positive value on the current state of bilateral relations and indicate that they will meet soon to explore possibilities of cooperation. This meeting took place in London on December 4 and 5, along with the second session of the Fishing Commission. In the joint communiqué, there is an agreement to establish a High Level Group with the mission of exploring the implications of the respective legislation on the continental shelf and the "possibilities of cooperation" in any of the activities derived from these measures.

The communiqué also notes the reciprocal reservation of the positions of the parties under the "sovereignty umbrella." Precisely because it is this way, it can go forward. The accords after Madrid III are a sample of what I suggested earlier concerning the division of maritime jurisdictions by subareas and also by jurisdictions. Negotiations are progressing rapidly on the right, though risky, road.

In addition, it is clear that these advances basically conform to the step-by-step approach proposed by the British administration. Mrs. Thatcher's position took on some flexibility while she was still prime minister, although according to various British writers this was particularly difficult because of her "dogmatic temperament that opposes any rapprochement" (S. 21, p. 149). But I believe there is no alternative for the time being to advancing little by little. We must work without haste but without pause, so that negotiations neither come to a standstill nor advance in response to the interests of only one of the parties.

The fact that since November 22, 1990, Margaret Thatcher has not been prime minister does not in and of itself open any visible way to the solution of the controversy. I have been explicit regarding the difficulties emanating from the attitude of the Islanders, with their powerful and articulate lobby and their increased confidence resulting from their new status and their solid economic position. Walter Little notes that these developments are not fully understood, but the general tendency "appears to reflect a greater desire of people to accept the status quo" (S. 31, p. 35).

It is more than that. While it was the Crown that regained, in 1986, the fishing rights it claimed over the renewable and nonrenewable fishing resources in the Malvinas, and more recently, in 1991, over the continental shelf, island authorities have been in charge of implementing these measures. The United Kingdom will presumably use this fact as an excuse to say, in negotiations with Argentina, that its hands are tied because the decision lies with the Kelpers. This is not true, because both measures were a mandate from the Crown, which fixed even the terms of reference.

All this makes one think that the road will be long and difficult. Whichever British administration is in power, I share the opinion of Walter Little that the great expenditures effected to restructure defense "will significantly increase the British commitment to the islands" (S. 14, p. 153). It will be necessary for both parties to exercise patience, moderation, and political realism. Peter Beck shares these conclusions. And he says a negotiated accommodation will require a reevaluation of each side's political interests, including its minimum and maximum objectives (S. 21, p. 163).

COLOPHON: A SOLUTION BASED ON THE
VITAL INTERESTS OF THE PARTIES

Assuming that the vital interests of Argentina in the Malvinas really were economic—the totality of renewable and nonrenewable resources of the maritime areas—a highly positive first step for the Argentines would be to exercise full jurisdiction over the sea and the continental shelf. But if we speak of flexibility in our position, at least in the first phase, jurisdiction will go only from continental Argentina to the islands. There are many ways to attain this first objective, but one of the least complex would be to divide sovereignty over the territory of the two principal islands of the Malvinas archipelago. The exercise of sovereignty over the more western island, that is Gran Malvina (West Falkland), would be recognized as Argentina's in the shortest possible time. The limit of the respective maritime areas (EEZ) between the two islands would be the meridian corresponding to the halfway point between both mouths, to the north and to the south, of the Strait of San Carlos (Falkland Sound). This would also obviate what we have already indicated as a complicated task: marking the limits of the territorial waters.

This agreement would allow Argentina to organize fishing policy and procedures over a very extended maritime area, and could open the way to drilling on the continental shelf, indispensable to evaluating the importance and economic viability of the nonrenewable resources of the region. We have already seen that the most important deposits lie between Gran Malvina and the Argentine coast, including Burdwood Bank.

Events since the end of 1991 and the rhythm of bilateral discussions regarding nonrenewable resources are a wake-up call, especially for

Argentina. It would be appropriate that licenses to conduct seismic exploration, which could include shallow drilling, be granted to both Argentine and British companies, perhaps as joint ventures, or at least so that the results might be shared. Only in this way would the involvement of industry, preferably the petroleum industry, be acceptable in an area with no marked limits, where demarcation could be very difficult because, in the legislation recently adopted by both parties, the respective claims of sovereignty overlap.

The High Level Group has had ideas for cooperation, but no agreements have been reached. The parties have agreed to inform their governments—that is, they have agreed to disagree. Still, the way is open to cooperation.

In early 1993, in response to the call for bids, Gecco Prakla and Espectrum corporations conducted seismic studies to the south and the north, respectively, in the seabed around the islands. In this connection, Foreign Minister Di Tella reiterated to the British government Argentina's refusal to recognize the political and juridical legitimacy of exploration for and exploitation of petroleum resources in the disputed area. Later he warned that the Foreign Ministry would initiate action against any company involved in such activity. For the time being, the directives of the companies named have stated that they preferred to cooperate with Argentine petroleum companies rather than engage in conflict with them.

At the same time, there are British investors interested in the privatization and the deregulation process that Argentina is currently experiencing. To cite one example, British Gas joined leading Argentine companies in the purchase of the METROGAS (Metropolitan Gas Distribution) corporate stock package. In another case, YPF corporation (a state-owned petroleum company in the process of privatization) decided to postpone bidding on certain areas, which included part of the sedimentary basin of the Malvinas, until new research could be carried out, which is inevitable in the zone with no defined boundaries. Perhaps private petroleum companies of both countries could conduct a "joint venture" (under the "umbrella" or without it).

Cooperation in economic activities implies a true partnership and would have no limits except that imposed by the willingness of the intervening parties to reach agreement. With regard to the income resulting from these activities, the island community must be duly considered within a "package" that reasonably takes care of the interests of all involved.

Regarding the legal-institutional regime, the conclusions reached by the British authors I have quoted on the possibilities of autonomy, which the national constitution allows the Argentine provinces, might be applicable to Gran Malvina. As Argentine delegations have reiterated since 1965, and a recent government declaration confirmed, this regime could be accompanied by an ad hoc statute of guaranties designed to preserve as far as possible the Kelpers' way of life. Those who wish could be indemnified and relocated, including on Soledad (East Falkland). Financially, the operation would not be costly because there are only some 150 families living on Gran Malvina.

As to Soledad, and its territorial seas, the agreement could include the option of a leaseback provision. This would provide for transfer of sovereignty to Argentina with a simultaneous lease to the United Kingdom for a long term of, say, two or more generations. Meanwhile, oil companies from both countries would be able to jointly conduct exploration and drilling to locate economically profitable wells.

Such a solution would allow the two parties to pursue their principal interest—sensible exploration of the region's natural resources—and at the same time buy time for the Kelpers to become accustomed to the new situation. As noted earlier, timing is of the essence. What seems insoluble today can, over time, be rendered soluble.

I am optimistic that this will be the case. In commenting on a public opinion poll taken in England in 1990, Walter Little notes that leaseback was a more difficult option to contemplate after the 1982 conflict than it had been before. And outright "handover" to Argentina, he concluded, "would provoke a political storm." Thus: "The most that could be sold politically would appear to be some option of internationalization or neutralization." (S. 31, pp. 65–66)

These options are unacceptable to Argentina, as Professor Little well knows, and so one might conclude that public opinion in the United Kingdom closes the door to any solution acceptable to both sides. I read the same poll somewhat differently, however, and take heart from the fact that 13 percent of those polled in the Labour Party favored transfer of sovereignty to Argentina, while 25 percent were in favor of negotiations that at least included the issue of sovereignty. In other words, there are already significant numbers of British citizens who are prepared at least to contemplate a change of status. I believe those numbers will grow as the realities of the unworkable status quo begin to bear in on thinking Britishers.

One reason that is so has to do with the burden of military expenditures over a long period of time. I would agree with Little and others who have noted that in the immediate wake of expending blood and treasure to regain the islands, the United Kingdom is, of course, less disposed to giving them up than it was before the conflict. In the same way, having invested in establishing a military complex at Mount Pleasant to defend the islands, the United Kingdom will not wish to give up that base in the near term. Those observations are true enough. The question is: Will the United Kingdom wish to continue indefinitely the burden of maintaining a defense force in the islands that outnumbers the inhabitants? Clearly, while

Argentina has no intention and no wish to resort again to force, until there is a solution to the sovereignty question, confrontation cannot be excluded as a future possibility. Does it make sense for the United Kingdom to maintain "Fortress Falklands" indefinitely, with all the expense that will entail, rather than arriving at some accommodation with Argentina? I think not.

Further, under the formula I have suggested above, in which East Falkland would remain under British control as part of a long-term lease, the United Kingdom could hold onto the Mount Pleasant complex as long as it wished—or at least until the lease ran out. The point, however, is that given the reduced tensions with Argentina, it could significantly scale back the numbers of military personnel involved and the expenditures to support them. Another possibility for the future would be joint control of the base, or even multilateral control.

Another problem whose solution I see as something of a sine qua non for ensuring a stable and permanent accommodation is the lifting of the immigration restriction in force in the Malvinas with respect to the Argentine citizens. This restriction is in flagrant violation of fundamental human rights and the established practices of civilized nations. Nothing justified its enforcement before the 1982 conflict and nothing justifies it now that diplomatic relations have been reestablished and every requisite for the movement of the citizens of the two countries has been provided. It should be lifted.

As to the South Georgia and South Sandwich archipelagoes, the fact that they are uninhabited territories permits the United Kingdom to handle them less emotionally and without the involvement of the island community.

Argentina in turn might want to adopt a more flexible position with regard to those two archipelagoes. For example, a condominium might be possible, such as that suggested in the Labour proposal of 1977.

Meanwhile, the rational exploitation of living resources in the extensive territorial waters of these archipelagoes is of utmost importance. Dangerously predatory practices were noted until the Convention on the Conservation of Antarctic Marine Living Resources (CCAMLR), signed in Canberra in 1979, became effective. Since then fishing has been regulated by one of its organs, the Commission, whose first meetings date back to 1982 and which includes representatives from Argentina and the United Kingdom.

The Commission has already adopted conservation measures. Under the CCAMLR however, Argentina and the United Kingdom could jointly regulate all activities in the territorial waters of the two archipelagoes that are not specifically regulated by the CCAMLR. This could include stricter conservation measures (such as quotas, fishing capture regulations, etc.). It would also include police power and the issuance of fishing licenses.

According to the formula contained in the last paragraph of the CCAMLR (see Appendix 5), a joint Anglo-Argentine declaration recovering possession of the Exclusive Economic Zone would be needed to put fishermen from third countries on notice that these maritime areas have an owner (or owners), an indispensable step in the licensing process.

This seems to me an attractive opportunity for coordinated action, and the benefits accruing to the two parties would be such that the option deserves to be explored early in the negotiating process.

On May 7, 1993, the British government announced measures extending its jurisdiction over the 200-mile radius of EEZ (its jurisdiction had previously been limited to 12 miles of territorial sea) around the South Georgias and the South Sandwich Islands, and reserving rights over the living and nonliving resources of both the waters and the seabed of the respective maritime zones. One must remember that in 1966 Argentina had adopted a general measure with relation to the maritime spaces adjacent to its continental and island territory, which was reiterated in 1991 in Law 23.968. Argentina considered the British decision, by referring specifically to the disputed archipelagoes, to be a gratuitously irritating gesture and rejected it through a note to the Foreign Office dated the same day.

However, two days later, at the suggestion of the United Kingdom, both governments issued a joint declaration in which they agreed on the need to strengthen the conservation measures adopted by the Commission of the CCAMLR. Both governments also agreed to communicate this joint declaration to the Commission and its members. And now that both parties have unilaterally declared a 200-mile EEZ, what will happen with the measures that they adopted together to avoid predatory fishing and its considerable environmental and ecological effects? Will they be respected by powerful fishing interests? Will Anglo-Argentine cooperation be limited to the preservation of the species? Or will the day come when we see fishing vessels operating in the archipelagoes under jointly issued licenses?

For the time being, clearly, all proposals to jointly regulate fishing, to issue licenses, or to otherwise agree on exploitation of the maritime resources in the region must be subject to the reservation of rights under the sovereignty umbrella. Under it, all sorts of agreements are possible without prejudice to the legal position of either side. Without it, not much progress is likely to be made. I believe it is inevitable that the day will come when by mutual agreement the two governments will close the umbrella and deal with the underlying sovereignty issue in a comprehensive way.

Both sides must be truly prepared to negotiate, and that implies a willingness to compromise on initial demands in a true *do ut des*. Peter Beck mentions an admonition of Lord Carrington to British politicians and mass media. His words are equally applicable, however, to their Argentine counterparts. I believe this admonition is sufficiently important to be quoted in full:

> There are individuals in Parliament and in the press who really seem to think that there is something dishonest or unworthy in trying to come to an agreement with a foreign government. It is their opinion that negotiating is a sign of weakness, even when the settling of a problem is in the interest of both parties and is proposed in order to prevent the occurrence of a situation prejudicial to the political and economic interests of the country. They take chauvinism to such heights that one almost feels they disapprove if someone in the Foreign Office speaks to a foreigner. Negotiation, as it were, is a sign of weakness and lack of patriotism. But the alternative to negotiation is confrontation . . . which is not in the interests of the country, is extremely costly and, often, in the long run ends in war. (S. 21, p. 163)

The formula I have outlined in Appendix 6 is the result of arranging the component pieces into a coherent mosaic and is a fair example of real willingness to negotiate. In July 1993, a solution to the dispute that would allow a great deal of autonomy to the islands' population was considered favorably by officials of the Argentine Chancellery, and in November 1993, Guido Di Tella, minister for foreign affairs, visited the Aland Islands to study in situ the evolution of an imaginative system developed by Finland and Sweden over half a century ago and still in force today. The Aland Islands agreement recognizes Finnish sovereignty, but gives political, juridical, and economic autonomy to the islands' (mostly Swedish) inhabitants.

This was the first time that the possibility of such an arrangement was seriously examined in the context of the Malvinas. Ultimately, Di Tella discarded it as unsuitable to the actual situation in the islands. But the "association" approach is ever present.

The most important issue is to find a solution that will ensure that peace and security acquire a permanent character, permitting—as Lord Carrington's admonition would have it—cooperation to replace confrontation, which will always be lurking in the wings until the sovereignty dispute is resolved.

Appendix 1

Amendments Proposed by the United Kingdom

United Nations
General Assembly

Distr.
Limited
A/40/L.20

Fortieth session
Agenda item 23

20 November 1985
Original: English

QUESTION OF THE FALKLAND ISLANDS (MALVINAS)

United Kingdom of Great Britain and Northern Ireland: Amendments to draft resolution A/40/L.19

1. *Insert* the following new second preambular paragraph:

"*Reaffirming* that in accordance with the Charter of the United Nations all people have the right to self-determination and by virtue of that right they freely determine their political status and freely pursue their economic, social and cultural development,"

2. At the end of operative paragraph 1 *add* the following:

"and the right thereunder of peoples to self-determination;"

Author's note : Submitted separately to a vote on November 27, 1985, these proposed amendments were rejected by the General Assembly with the following result:

- First amendment: 38 votes in favor, 60 against, and 43 abstentions.
- Second amendment: 36 votes in favor, 57 against, and 48 abstentions.

Appendix 2

Memorandum of Understanding on the Question of the Falkland Islands

Secret
8/18/68

1. Representatives of the Government of the United Kingdom of Great Britain and Northern Ireland and of the government of the Argentine Republic having held discussions regarding the question of the Falkland Islands (Islas Malvinas) in a friendly and cooperative spirit, in accordance with Resolution 2065 (XX) of the United Nations, have recorded in this Memorandum their understanding of the position reached in their discussions.

2. The common objective is to settle definitively and in an amicable manner the dispute over sovereignty, taking duly into account the interests of the population of the islands. In order to create conditions in which this objective can be achieved the two Governments intend to make early progress with practical measures to promote freedom of communication and movement between the mainland and the islands, in both directions, in such a way as to encourage the development of cultural, economic and other links.

3. To that effect and in a desire to contribute towards such a settlement, the Government of the Argentine Republic will promote free communication and movement between the mainland and the islands and the United Kingdom Government will collaborate in the implementation of this policy. Discussions on the practical measures to be adopted will now take place in Buenos Aires.

4. The Government of the United Kingdom as part of such a final settlement will recognize Argentina's sovereignty over the islands from a date to be agreed. This date will be agreed as soon as possible after (i) the

two Governments have resolved the present divergence between them as to the criteria according to which the United Kingdom Government shall consider whether the interests of the Islanders would be secured by the safeguards and guarantees to be offered by the Argentine Government and (ii) the Government of the United Kingdom are then satisfied that those interests are so secured.

5. Both Governments will proceed with the present talks in London in order to define the details of the guarantees and safeguards for the interests of the population of the islands to be put forward by the Argentine Government.

6. The two Governments have taken note of each others' policies and share the view that a certain period of time should facilitate the development of conditions for a definitive settlement. If no definitive settlement had been reached, a meeting of special representatives could be held at the request of either Government to review progress or to examine the question at a date of not less than four years or not more than ten years from the signature of this Memorandum.

Appendix 3

Application of the Declaration on the Concession of Independence to Colonial Countries and Peoples

United Nations
General Assembly

Distr.
General
A/32/111
9 June 1977

Thirty-second session
Agenda item 24

Spanish
Original: English

*Letter dated June 8, 1977, addressed to the
Secretary General by the Permanent Representative to the
United Nations from Great Britain and Northern Ireland.*

I have the honor of addressing Your Excellency with respect to the question of the Falkland Islands and, in keeping with paragraph 5 of Resolution 31/49 of the General Assembly, of December 1, 1976, of delivering a copy of the joint communiqué released in London and Buenos Aires April 26, 1977.

I request that Your Excellency please have this letter and its attachment distributed as a document of the General Assembly and call it to the attention of the Special Committee on Decolonization.

Ivor Richard

ATTACHMENT

The Governments of the Argentine Republics and the United Kingdom of Great Britain and Northern Ireland have agreed to hold negotiations from

June or July 1977 which will concern future political relations, including sovereignty with regard to the Falkland Islands, South Georgia and South Sandwich Islands, and economic co-operation with regard to the said territories, in particular, and the South West Atlantic, in general. In these negotiations the issues affecting the future of the islands will be discussed and negotiations will be directed to the working out of a peaceful solution to the existing dispute on sovereignty between the two states, and the establishment of a framework for Anglo-Argentine economic co-operation which will contribute substantially to the development of the islands, and the region as a whole.

A major objective of the negotiations will be to achieve a stable, prosperous and politically durable future for the islands, whose people the Government of the United Kingdom will consult during the course of the negotiations.

The agreement to hold these negotiations, and the negotiations themselves, are without prejudice to the position of either Government with regard to sovereignty over the islands.

The level at which the negotiations will be conducted, and the times and places at which they will be held, will be determined by agreement between the two Governments. If necessary, special Working Groups will be established.

Appendix 4

Area of Application of the Joint Declaration on the Conservation of Fishing Resources (Madrid, 11/28/90)

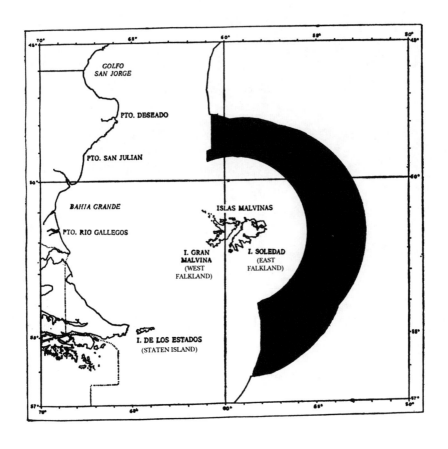

Appendix 5

Declaration on the Application of the Convention on the Conservation of Antarctic Living Marine Resources, Canberra, 7–20 May 1980: Final Act

Statement made by the Chairman on 19 May 1980 regarding the application of the Convention on the Conservation of Antarctic Living Marine Resources to the waters adjacent to Kerguelen and Crozet over which France has jurisdiction, and to waters adjacent to other islands within the area to which this Convention applies over which the existence of State sovereignty is recognized by all contracting Parties.

1. Measures for the conservation of Antarctic marine living resources of the waters adjacent to Kerguelen and Crozet, over which France has jurisdiction, adopted by France prior to the entry in force of the Convention, would remain in force after the entry into force of the Convention until modified by France acting within the framework of the Convention or otherwise.

2. After the Convention has come into force, each time the Commission should undertake examination of the conservation needs of the marine living resources of the general area in which waters adjacent to Kerguelen and Crozet are to be found, it would be open to France either to agree that the waters in question should be included in the area of application of any specific conservation measure under consideration or to indicate that they should be excluded. In the latter event, the Commission would not proceed to the adoption of the specific conservation measure in a form applicable to the waters in question unless France removed its objection to it. France could also adopt such national measures as it might deem appropriate for the waters in question.

3. Accordingly, when specific conservation measures are considered within the framework of the Commission and with the participation of France, then:

    (a) France would be bound by any conservation matters adopted by consensus with its participation for the duration of those measures. This would not prevent France from promulgating national measures that were more strict than the Commission's measures or which dealt with other matters;

    (b) In the absence of consensus, France could promulgate any national measures which it might deem appropriate.

4. Conservation measures, whether national measures or measures adopted by the Commission, in respect of the waters adjacent to Kerguelen and Crozet, would be enforced by France. The system of observation and inspection foreseen by the Convention would not be implemented in the waters adjacent to Kerguelen and Crozet except as agreed by France and in the manner so agreed.

5. *The understandings, set forth in paragraphs 1–4 above, regarding the application of the Convention to waters adjacent to the Islands of Kerguelen and Crozet, also apply to waters adjacent to the islands within the area to which this convention applies over which the existence of State sovereignty is recognized by all Contracting Parties* (emphasis added).

Appendix 6

The Malvinas Question: Territories and Maritime Jurisdictions, Asymmetric Scheme

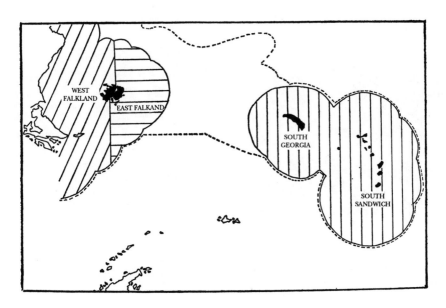

- - - - - - - - - Outer edge of the continental shelf

/// Gran Malvina (West Falkland) with its EEZ and shelf: Recognition of Argentine sovereignty within the briefest possible time period

Isla Soledad (East Falkland) with its EEZ and shelf: Preservation of British institutions for a prolonged period (leaseback) and/or delay of any accord for the duration of the period agreed upon by both parties

||| South Georgia and South Sandwich with their respective maritime areas: Condominium over the territories or joint administration; EEZ and shelf: Joint administration

British Texts Cited

S. 1.   *Falkland Islands Review*. Report of the Committee chaired by Lord Franks, presented in Parliament by Margaret Thatcher. January 1983.

S. 2.   Report of the Foreign Relations Committee of the House of Commons, chaired by Sir Kershaw. Academic research. Published January 17, 1983.

S. 3.   Falkland Islands. Summaries of testimony taken in the islands by the Kershaw Committee on February 3, 4, and 7, 1983. Published by the House of Commons, February 14, 1983.

S. 4.   House of Commons. Minutes of the proceedings of the Kershaw Committee, 1982–1983 session. First draft report, "A policy for the Falkland Islands." Published May 11, 1983.

S. 5.   House of Commons. Testimony before the Kershaw Committee, 1983–1984 session, vol. 2.

S. 6.   Report of the Foreign Relations Committee of the House of Commons, "A Policy for the Falkland Islands." Published October 25, 1984, vol. 2.

S. 7.   Samuel Johnson, LL.D. *Thoughts on the Late Transactions Respecting Falkland Islands*. 1771. Reprinted. Essex: Thames Bank Publishing, 1948.

S. 8.   Julius Goebel (U.S. citizen). *The Struggle for the Falkland Islands*. New Haven: Yale University Press, 1927.

S. 9.   Peter J. Beck. "Cooperative Confrontation in the Falkland Islands Dispute: The Anglo-Argentine Search for a Way Forward 1968–1981." *Journal of Inter-American Studies and World Affairs* 24, no. 1 (February 1982).

S. 10.   Denzil Dunnett. "Self-determination and the Falklands." *International Affairs* 59, no. 3 (Summer 1983).

S. 11.   Peter J. Beck. "The Anglo-Argentine Dispute over Title to the Falkland Islands: Changing British Perceptions on Sovereignty Since 1910." *Millennium Journal of International Studies* 12, no. 1 (Spring 1983).

S. 12.   William Wallace (director of studies, Chatham House). "How Frank Was Franks?" *International Affairs* 59, no. 3 (Summer 1983).

S. 13.   Peter J. Beck. "Britain's Falklands Future: The Need to Look Back." *Round Table*, no. 290 (1984), Butterworth and Co.

S. 14.   Walter Little. "Anglo-Argentine Relations and the Management of the Falklands Question." *British Foreign Policy Under Thatcher.* P. Byrd and P. Allan, 1988.

S. 15.   Michael Stephen (secretary of the Foreign Relations Committee of the Bow Group). *The Falklands: A Possible Way Forward.* London: Bow Publications, 1984.

S. 16.   C. R. Mitchell. *Alternative Approaches to the Issue of Sovereignty in the Falklands/Malvinas Dispute.* London: The City University, 1984.

S. 17.   Ambassador Nicholas Henderson. "The Falklands Dimension." *Washington Post*, January 23, 1983.

S. 18.   Jeffrey D. Mhyre. "Title to the Falklands-Malvinas Under International Law." *Millennium Journal of International Studies* 12, no. 1 (Spring 1983).

S. 19.   Peter Calvert. "Sovereignty and the Falklands Crisis." *International Affairs* 59, no. 3 (Summer 1983).

S. 20.   Peter J. Beck. "Research Problems in Studying Britain's Latin American Past: The Case of the Falklands Dispute 1920–1950." *Bulletin of Latin American Research* 2, no. 2 (May 1983).

S. 21.   Peter J. Beck. *The Falkland Islands as an International Problem.* Routledge, 1988.

S. 22.   Peter J. Beck. "Britain's Antarctic Dimension." House of Commons. Published 1984. P. 444.

S. 23.   Joan Pearce. *The Falkland Islands Dispute: International Dimensions. The Falkland Islands Negotiations, 1965–82.* London: Royal Institute of International Affairs, 1982.

S. 24.   Bonafacio del Carril. *La cuestión de las Malvinas.* Buenos Aires: Emecé, 1983.

S. 25.   Ferrer Vieyra. *An Annotated Legal Chronology on the Malvinas (Falkland) Islands Controversy.* Cordoba: Marcos Lerner, 1985.

S. 26.   Diego García, Minority Rights Group Report. Sessions Diary of the House of Lords. Vol. 436, no. 5, 397–401.

S. 27.   Wilfred Down. *The Occupation of the Falkland Islands and the Question of Sovereignty.* Cambridge University, 1927.

S. 28. Professor J. C. J. Metford. "Falklands or Malvinas? The Background of the Dispute." *International Affairs* 44 (1968).

S. 29. David Thomas. "The View from Whitehall." In *Toward Resolution? The Falklands/Malvinas Dispute,* edited by Wayne S. Smith. Boulder: Lynne Rienner Publishers, 1991.

S. 30. Jack Speyer. Panel of Foreign Affairs. Commission for Latin America. Liberal Party. London, 1984.

S. 31. Walter Little. "Political Opinion in Britain." In *Toward Resolution? The Falklands/Malvinas Dispute,* edited by Wayne S. Smith. Boulder: Lynne Rienner Publishers, 1991.

About the Book and Author

This unusual analysis of the Falkland/Malvinas dispute relies almost entirely on British sources to refute British claims to the islands.

Oliveri López draws on official government documents, speeches, works of scholarship, and statements by residents of the islands themselves to substantiate his conclusion of "admission" by the United Kingdom of Argentine sovereignty over the Malvinas. Presenting his own view of the interests of the southern archipelagoes, he also explores various options for future negotiations regarding the region.

A career diplomat, **Angel M. Oliveri López** joined the Argentine Foreign Service in 1956. In 1973–1978 he served as minister plenipotentiary in the Permanent Mission of Argentina to the United Nations, and in 1978–1981 he headed the Antarctica and Malvinas section of the Argentine foreign ministry. He has also served as Ambassador to Czechoslovakia, undersecretary of international economic negotiations, and permanent representative to the Latin America Association for Integration (ALADI). Ambassador Oliveri López is the author of *Economic Integration and International Law.*